Praise for *Co-Active Coaching*, Fourth Edition

"With its fourth updated edition, *Co-Active Coaching* remains the bible of coaching guides. Written with a powerful, distinctive approach, no other book gives you the tools, the skills, and the fundamentals needed to succeed in these delicate relationships."

—Stephen R. Covey, Author, *The 7 Habits of Highly Effective People* and *The Leader in Me*

"In *Co-Active Coaching*, the dynamic Kimsey-House duo, along with Phillip Sandahl, have elevated coaching from an instructional tool to an art form! Seldom have I seen such a clear road map for how to 'overcome actions that sabotage desires, plans and dreams.' Collaboration, cooperation, coalition—all necessary components of a successful working relationship. As a gym coach leads his trainee to a higher state of physical health and wellbeing, *Co-Active Coaching* provides business coaches with a toolkit for helping their clients achieve professional and personal success. *Co-Active Coaching* should be required reading for every manager or employee who wants to succeed in the workplace."

—Marshall Goldsmith, Two Million-Selling Author, *New York Times* Bestsellers *Triggers, MOJO* and *What Got You Here Won't Get You There*

"*Co-Active Coaching* exudes the catalytic power to transform your organization and your life. Read it, savor it, and practice it to become a purpose-filled leader of life! "

—Kevin Cashman, Best-Selling Author, *Leadership from the Inside Out* and *The Pause Principle*

"I applaud the new edition of this definitive text on transformational coaching. The authors and the visionary network they lead provide an effective methodology to work with change at personal and organizational levels. This is a must-read for professionals who value the process of discovery, awareness, and choice that empowers people to find their own inner wisdom and to act in service to make a better world for all."

—Lynne Twist, Author, *The Soul of Money*, Founder, Soul of Money Institute, and Co-Founder, The Pachamama Alliance

"*Co-Active Coaching* insightfully reveals how to unlock a person's potential and enlighten their past, present, and future. It's a must-read for all self-empowered senior executives."

    —Michael Cheah, Former President, Xian-Janssen Pharmaceutical, China
    (A Johnson & Johnson Group of Companies)

"Transformational change—in ourselves or in the teams, organizations, and companies we lead—is ultimately all about relationships. The fourth edition of *Co-Active Coaching*, by the eloquent and compassionate founders of the Co-Active Training Institute, will give you the tools, skills, strategies, and ethical frameworks to achieve the powerful goals of this work: changing lives and changing the world."

    —Celeste Schenck, President, The American University of Paris

"Coaching basics are an essential skill set for any manager or leader who is interested in developing other people, so I use this material in most of the MBA courses I teach. Without fail, it engages the hearts and minds of people who care about acquiring meaningful and effective skills they can immediately put to use."

    —Heidi Brooks, PhD, Director, Yale School of Management Mentoring Program,
    Lecturer, Yale School of Management, and Clinical Assistant Professor, Yale School
    of Medicine, Department of Psychiatry

"*Co-Active Coaching*, Fourth Edition is a must read for any leader who wants to personally perform higher and take their team to a higher level of performance, regardless of culture. Having lived and worked in the Middle East for the past two decades, this book transcends culture, religion and ethnicity and connects to who we are as human beings."

    —Kevin Craig - Founder of Craig Consultants and Co-Founder of Grip Arabia.
    Co-Author of *Polar Bears and Penguins*. High Performance, Executive and Leadership
    Co-Active Coach, Kingdom of Bahrain

"The principles offered in *Co-Active Coaching* have fostered a journey that has genuinely shifted our organizational culture. Nowhere is this clearer than with job satisfaction and retention. My people love coming to work every day and they drive each other to be an even better version of themselves on behalf of our organizational mission. Together, we work to infuse Co-Active methodologies throughout Colorado's Child Welfare System with great success!"

—Kasey Matz, Director, Colorado Child Welfare Training System

"Our company, AFCC Automotive Fuel Cell Cooperation, embarked upon our CTI Co-Active inspired coaching journey, creating an extraordinary coaching culture. Using the models and tools outlined in this book, we utilize coaching discussions in many aspects of our business and employ Co-Active CTI-based principles across our company. Our journey culminated when AFCC was awarded the British Columbia Prism award, followed by the ICF Global Prism award in 2017!"

—Jim Boerger, Director of Operations

"*Co-Active Coaching* has already touched thousands of Japanese hearts with its first three editions. I am utterly convinced that the content of this book transcends the cultural boundaries because it speaks to something that we universally share as human beings. Now that its fourth edition is out, I can only feel excited when I imagine how many more hearts will be touched around the globe!"

—Hide Enemoto, Founder, CTI Japan

"Schouten & Nelissen is a proud partner of CTI, and we feel privileged to spread this wonderful and important work throughout the world. *Co-Active Coaching* has not only changed the lives of many, it has also touched the hearts of all coaches in our communities in the Netherlands, Belgium, Luxembourg, Germany, Switzerland and China."

—Marcel van Bronswijk, Board President, Schouten Global

"As an R&D manager in today's high-tech companies, I was facing an ever-increasing demand for emotional intelligence and support for employee's development. *Co-Active Coaching* has unlocked the gifts of true listening and empathy, turning me into a better person and a better manager. This book an excellent companion for any manager who wishes to follow the path of co-active coaching for personal and professional growth."

—Adi Sapir, VP of Research and Development, Israeli high tech company

CO-ACTIVE
COACHING

The proven framework for transformative conversations at work and in life

FOURTH EDITION

Henry Kimsey-House

Karen Kimsey-House

Phillip Sandahl

and

Laura Whitworth

NICHOLAS BREALEY
PUBLISHING

BOSTON · LONDON

This edition first published in 2018 by Nicholas Brealey Publishing

An imprint of John Murray Press

An Hachette company

24 23 22 21 20 19 18   1 2 3 4 5 6 7 8 9 10

A CIP catalogue record for this title is available from the British Library

Library of Congress Control Number: 2018902737

ISBN 978-1-47367-498-1
US eBook ISBN 978-1-47369-112-4
UK eBook ISBN 978-1-47369-113-1

Printed and bound in the United States of America

John Murray Press policy is to use papers that are natural, renewable, and recyclable products and made from wood grown in sustainable forests. The logging and manufacturing processes are expected to conform to the environmental regulations of the country of origin.

John Murray Press Ltd
Carmelite House
50 Victoria Embankment
London EC4Y 0DZ
Tel: 020 3122 6000

Nicholas Brealey Publishing
Hachette Book Group
Market Place Center, 53 State Street
Boston, MA 02109, USA
Tel: (617) 523 3801

www.nbuspublishing.com

Contents

Preface to the Fourth Edition

O n one hand, the title of the book says everything you need to know in terms of what this book is about: co-active coaching. After 20 years and three editions we still emphasize *coaching*, which is our heritage, our expertise, and our learning laboratory, but now we also highlight what it means to be *co-active*, and it is that expanded emphasis that is the fundamental reason for the fourth edition. We will look especially at how being *co-active* applies to—and empowers—conversations that don't fit a traditional coaching form. It's a shift in focus based on an awareness of how fundamentally conversations are changing and why an understanding of what it means to be in a *"co-active" conversation* is so important and so fitting in the world of work today.

In simple terms, *coaching* describes what we *do*. This book presents a robust model for coaching; principles, methodologies, and contexts for coaching; and practical skills for coaching. In other words, it's about how to do coaching effectively. We have been pioneers in the field of coaching and have trained tens of thousands of co-active coaches around the world.

Co-active is about the nature of the coaching *relationship*. It involves how the coach and the coachee work together—the alliance—for the sake of the coachee's agenda. That underlying co-active relationship has been featured in previous editions and is essential to an understanding of what makes this coaching approach unique and transformative. The key word there is *underlying*.

As we considered revisions for this edition, we realized that the nature of the environment in which coaching takes place—or where informal coach-like conversations take place—needs to have more visibility. What *co-active* contributes is the container for effective conversation, and that container is as important as the coaching conversation itself. Given the changing nature of the world we live and work in, it is clear there is an urgent need to highlight this fundamental aspect of the work. The ground conditions necessary for sustainable and transformative change in all coaching relationships, whether formal or informal, come from the act of consciously creating *co-active* relationships: relationships that are collaborative, cooperative, co-created, active, and engaged and that yield action steps and learning. Consequently, this book focuses on the context for effective coaching: creating the container.

The fact that a coaching approach has been adapted to conversations beyond the scope of the professional coach and coachee isn't new. We made that observation years ago in the second edition, where we noted how the basic skills and mind-set of co-active coaching have been applied to conversations that aren't in a structured coaching format: the private, one-on-one conversation between a trained coach and a coachee. For example, we considered the skills of coaching applied by teachers working with students; healthcare staff working with patients; and managers, supervisors, and team leaders learning how to adapt the fundamentals of coaching to empower and support others who were not "coachees" but who participated in relationships that provided a fitting opportunity for a coach-like conversation.

What has shifted subtly over time is that the very nature of conversation has changed. Step outside the world of coaching and you will see the evidence. Take a glance at your phone—something that didn't exist when this book was first published. (The first iPhone and the second edition of *Co-Active Coaching* both appeared in 2007.) A great deal of what's possible in communication today would have qualified as science fiction when the first edition of this book was published. On a cultural and relationship level, what's possible would have been dismissed as "not in our lifetime," and yet here we are.

Today it is easy to communicate with colleagues, family, and friends instantly across the globe. Technology has had an enormous impact on how we can communicate and with whom. And yet the lightning speed and range of connections available to us all pose their own issues. We can function more quickly, but can we connect as deeply as we need to? More than ever, the co-active skills of deep listening, shared commitment, and empowered learning are critical.

As you look for changes in conversations, also listen to the content. The norms for what we talk about and who is included in the conversation have evolved, opened up. This shift reflects a world more visibly diverse and distributed and yet more closely connected. It's also a world moving and shifting at an accelerated rate. We don't really notice because we're in it, just as we do not notice we are on a globe spinning at 900 miles an hour. Topics of conversation that would have seemed impossible or taboo a decade ago are now commonplace.

Given those conditions, it makes sense that coaching—with its inherent strengths for effective conversation—grew in a parallel way. Since the first edition, we have witnessed the dramatic spread of coaching globally: both the formal training and impact of professional coaches and the informal growth of the fundamentals of effective coaching conversations. Today the *co-active* part of our title is more important and more valuable than ever before.

Organizations have come to understand that effective performance depends on effective relationships. That awareness is changing how business gets done and how conversations move business forward. For leaders and managers, the ability to interact with employees by using a "coach approach" is now widely regarded as a core competency, an essential skill set. More and more, businesses see coaching as an invaluable tool in the development of talent, both in the formal coaching relationships and in the informal coaching roles that leaders and managers play with the people they lead.

Since the publication of the first edition, we have observed, learned, and adapted our work to needs in the profession of coaching and the environments where coaching takes place. At the time of the third edition, we saw a key role for coaching in a world going through fundamental realignment. The structure of organizations was changing from vertical and hierarchical (top down) to horizontal, dispersed, matrixed. We saw *Co-Active Coaching* as the means to have more effective change conversations, an approach that led to the book's subtitle.

As it turns out, what we observed happening in organizations was a reflection of what was happening in global culture. This fourth edition weaves that awareness into the discussion of what it means to create a co-active environment that supports open and transformative conversation, whether the situation involves a formal coaching relationship or important, informal conversations in leadership roles or between colleagues.

Over the years we have seen the evolution of our work and how it has influenced and been adapted as a leadership skill set and, perhaps more important, a leadership mind-set. The relationship infrastructure for effective organizational performance requires the skills and mind-set for a world that is increasingly reverberating with change.

Our goal is not for everyone to become coaches but to understand and be able to apply the fundamentals of an empowering coaching container. This fourth edition of *Co-Active Coaching* provides a new way to be in relationship while being in conversation—a way to understand and apply basic understanding of how these skills can support more effective results, transformative change, and healthier relationships both locally and globally.

This book is absolutely a continuation of our work with our roots in the fundamentals of one-on-one coaching. It also reflects our understanding that there is more to that impact than the coaching form itself. It explores the compelling way that being in relationship shows up in conversation and how conversation is more than words.

We believe this fourth edition of *Co-Active Coaching* meets the evolving needs of professional coaches, leaders in organizations, and all those who value effective relationship conversations. There is a way to create that container—a conscious framework in which empowered conversations can take place. Let's begin.

Acknowledgments

We owe an enormous debt of gratitude to so many people who have supported, encouraged, and championed this work—far too many to name, some we have never met. They represent all of the coaches and coachees who have embarked on a coaching journey; their lives and work are a living acknowledgment and a powerful motivation to keep this material current and meaningful.

Coaching training played an enormous role in spreading the power and possibility of coaching as a profession and became its own learning laboratory for what works in coaching. The faculty and staff of the Co-Active Training Institute have been at the forefront of the mission to prepare new coaches, maintain high professional standards, and keep the co-active method thriving. Their commitment to the essence and the particulars has helped us continuously refine what we present, and their contribution shows in this fourth edition.

We have seen coaching spread around the globe in the years since the first edition was published. Clearly there is a hunger in the world that is pulling coaching into organizations, relationships, and individual lives—something that transcends all of the usual boundaries. We want to especially acknowledge those courageous pioneers at the forefront of the global efforts. It would not happen without the vision and initiative of determined people willing to take on the challenge of language and culture for the sake of coaching.

To the thousands of coaching students we have trained, to our own coachees, and, yes, our own coaches, we are thankful beyond words. To all of the committed organizations, for their vision and courage to take a stand for human potential and for their dedication to creating co-active cultures we offer thanks as well. And finally, to the coachees who are and have always been our most important teachers, this acknowledgment is for you. You are the reason we do this work.

For Laura Whitworth

And finally, a very special acknowledgment for the life, pioneering work, and indomitable spirit of Laura Whitworth, one of the three original founders of CTI with Karen and Henry Kimsey-House. Laura was a visionary and one of earliest people to call herself a coach. She helped launch the profession and was a fierce advocate for the transformative potential of the co-active way. Her impact reverberates throughout this book.

Henry and Karen Kimsey-House
Phillip Sandahl

Introduction

Welcome to our *co-active* world—a world devoted to creating transformative conversations. We have our roots in professional coaching, so this is a book about a model, principles, contexts, and skills of coaching. The book represents more than 25 years of experience training people in how to be effective coaches through the Co-Active Training Institute (CTI), using the model and approach of co-active coaching. Today, CTI is the largest in-person coach training organization in the world, delivering courses in North America, Europe, the Middle East, and Asia.

This book describes the model in detail, defines the skills and techniques of co-active coaching, and offers sample coaching conversations and practical exercises all designed to help you understand and practice coaching—or have conversations that are based on co-active coaching fundamentals.

It's the second, broader application of co-active coaching that is behind this fourth edition. We were pioneers in the early development of coaching as a profession and have contributed to the vision, practice, and credibility of coaching as a professional competency. At the same time, more and more as the years progressed we have witnessed the essence of this work expand beyond the private dialogue between one professionally trained coach and one coachee. This book shines a brighter light on those important but informal coaching-influenced conversations.

Co-active coaching as a form is a particular way to be in conversation. It offers a unique way to listen, explore, raise awareness, make choices—in fact, take risks—and, always, to build on what was learned along the way to inform the next choice, the next step, and the next learning opportunity.

What we teach professional coaches is being adapted for conversations initiated by teachers, healthcare workers, and parents; more than anywhere else, what we teach is becoming an essential leadership competency for executives, managers, and supervisors.

We are not abandoning our roots. This book continues to be the most required or recommended book on the subject of coaching for business schools, college and university classes, and training programs worldwide. What has been added are more examples of coach-like conversations—examples of the power inherent in a dedication to the underlying principles of being in a *co-active* conversation.

Getting to the Core of Co-Active

This book is about the nature of a coaching relationship—specifically, a co-active relationship. We look at the nature of a co-active conversation and at what makes this so different from other conversations—whether the conversation is between a professional coach and coachee, or between a senior manager and that person's direct report. The heart of that conversation is the same when we look through the lens of the co-active way.

Here's the difference. In our view, coaching is not about solving problems, although problems will be solved. It is not primarily about improving performance, attaining goals, or achieving results, although all of that will certainly happen over time in an effective co-active coaching relationship. We believe that coaching is chiefly about discovery, awareness, and choice. It is a way of effectively empowering people to find their own answers, encouraging and supporting them on the path as they continue to make important choices.

Now imagine you're a team leader in a conversation with one of the team about the status of a mission-critical project. There are many ways to have that conversation. One way—a traditional way for a team leader—would be to ask for a report, analyze the situation, and then provide work direction. That might still be the way the conversation could go.

Here's a different way—a way that is more co-active, collaborative. For the team leader it involves empowering the team member (who may be much closer to the actual issues on a day-to-day basis), possibly brainstorming alternative action steps, and agreeing on a course of action. In this way the nature of the relationship shifts; the context for the conversation is more inclusive and more empowering. This is not meant to imply that one way is inherently better than the other. It is an invitation to see there is a choice and each has a different impact. There is, in fact, a broader palette, a wider range of leadership responses available.

In this fast-paced world of work, the pressure is on to create more engaged, more proactive, and more empowered employees. Waiting for a higher authority or escalating decision making impedes teams and organizations that need the agility to respond to often chaotic and complex choices. Creating and supporting a co-active way of working together delivers on the imperative and creates a culture of resilience and resourcefulness.

A co-active conversation has inherent ground rules regarding certain qualities that must be present: respect, openness, compassion, empathy, and a rigorous commitment to speaking the truth. There are certain assumptions underlying the conversation as well. We assume strength and capability, not weakness, helplessness, or dependence. We assume a deep desire to give the best and achieve potential. A co-active conversation has certain beliefs built into it: that every situation has possibilities and that people really do have the power of choice.

This is a way of being in relationship and being in conversation that shifts the focal point of the conversation from who has rank to what is possible. It shifts the conversation from simply analyzing and problem solving to working together more effectively and learning to be more resourceful so that future issues are actually easier to address because the relationship is resilient and creative.

This way of communicating is finding root not only in formal coaching relationships but in the workplace as a leadership style, and in teams and families as well. It works because it taps into a human need for collaborative, co-active conversation, which is so different from the usual authoritarian, superior/inferior experience based on roles and entrenched positions. In this growing awareness of "We are in this together," the conversation shifts to a place of common purpose searching for possibilities.

We see this every day in the work we do. Co-active coaching has taken root around the world, transcending historical cultural barriers because it connects at a deeply human level—at a place of longing for meaningful connection. From a global perspective we see this as part of an evolving human consciousness. We believe co-active conversations are both an example of this shift in human consciousness and an instrument to create it.

This unique style of co-active communication is visible in a variety of ways. You can see it in how a coach (or a person in a coaching role) listens: not only to the words but also to what is behind the words and even to the spaces between the words. You can see it in leaders who put as much value on openly listening as they do taking a stand for a point of view. Leaders who truly listen as coaches tune in to the nuances of voice, emotion, and energy; they listen for what is being said and what is not being said. They listen to the very best in others, even when the others can't hear it in themselves.

It's no coincidence that *active* is built into the name and the title for this book. Whether we're describing a co-active coaching relationship or a less formal conversation between colleagues at work, we focus attention on accountability. We value it not as a test or from a nagging, policing perspective but as an opportunity to harvest all the learning from what happened or didn't happen. That shift from judgment to learning is at the heart of a co-active conversation.

This emphasis on the combination of relationship and action is elegantly captured in the words for this form: it is co-active. It combines both being and doing: being collaborative, cooperating, working together on a mutual mission—and actively moving forward to a vision or goal.

With this book, you will learn new ways to work with others: how to discover and promote their mission, purpose, and specific agenda. You'll find effective ways to rigorously hold others to account in the spirit and commitment of learning. From a one-on-one coaching perspective, you'll discover a co-active approach to values, goal setting, life balance, and self-management, and you'll learn how it can apply in leadership roles as well.

You'll also learn strategies for addressing the self-limiting behavior that often shows up most strongly just when people need the courage to take risks for the sake of change or when it feels like there is a great deal at stake professionally for team members or leaders. These proven strategies help people stay on track and overcome actions that sabotage desires, plans, and dreams.

This book emphasizes information and exercises for professional coaches, yet the skills and insights it offers can be applied in almost any relationship—at work, with family and friends, on teams, in volunteer and community settings—because coaching skills and the nature of the relationship are not limited to professional coaching sessions. We recognize that the essence of coaching is now an adapted communication style growing beyond the skill set of professional coaches.

How the Book Is Structured

Part 1 presents an overview of the co-active coaching model. The first chapter starts with the four cornerstones that form the foundation on which the model is built. Together they form an interrelated net in which powerful conversations can occur. We go on to build the model with the introduction of the five contexts of co-active coaching: listening, intuition, curiosity, forwarding action and deepening learning, and self-management. We look at how these five show up in informal conversations as well.

The chapter also describes the three principles—fulfillment, balance, and process—that together form the coachee's focus at the heart of the model. Part 1 also explains how to design an effective working relationship between coach and coachee (what we call the "designed alliance") and how that practice can build trust in any working relationship.

Part 2 describes each of the five contexts in detail and presents descriptions and examples of the coaching skills in action. Here we provide sample coaching conversations as well as exercises that bring the skills to life. You'll find sample conversations from both perspectives: the professional coach and workplace examples.

Part 3 covers the three core principles: fulfillment, balance, and process. Each of the three principles provides a gateway for meaningful change for coaches, including employees who are working in informal coaching relationships with managers and leaders. Examples of coaching conversations in each chapter illustrate how the principle unfolds in actual practice. We also explore how the three principles are always in the background of any important leadership conversation.

Part 4 integrates the content that precedes it and provides a vision for coaching—especially co-active conversation—for the future. In a way, this final section resembles the completion of any coaching session: pulling the pieces together, then moving into action and the next steps on the journey.

In a way there is also a "part 5" if you include the Co-Active Online Toolkit (*coactive.com/toolkit*). With each edition of *Co-Active Coaching* we have included extensive coaching tools you can use and adapt for work with your coachees. Starting with the third edition, those tools were made available online where it was easy to add and update materials. Since the third edition that online toolkit has grown extensively and now includes audio and video elements as well. In the book you will find references to the online toolkit with suggestions for accessing specific tools.

In summary, this fourth edition offers a deeper understanding of the nature of an effective co-active relationship and provides the skills necessary to create and support one. The book provides a systematic structure reinforced with real-life examples and practical exercises for developing your coaching abilities. It is a book for those who want to expand their knowledge and develop their capacities as professional coaches and for those who wish simply to add a "co-active way" to important conversations using this unique, inclusive, and proven method we call *co-active coaching*.

Co-Active Fundamentals

From day one, coaching focuses on the coachee. People participate in or seek out coaching because they want things to be different. They are looking for change or they have important goals to reach. They may be motivated to write a book, to start a business, to make a leap up the career ladder, to have a healthier body. They come to coaching in order to be more effective or more satisfied in life and work; they come to develop new skills to help navigate life's changes.

Sometimes people want more from life: more peace of mind, more security, more impact in their work. And sometimes they want less: less confusion, less stress, less financial pressure. In general, they come to coaching because they want a better quality of life—more fulfillment, better balance—or a different process for accomplishing their desires. Whatever the individual reason, it all starts with a stirring of motivation within the coachee.

Part I explains what the coach brings to this interaction and shows what the process looks like from a co-active perspective. In this part of the book, we outline the elements and convey a sense of how they fit together in a comprehensive model. In later chapters, we expand on these major components to provide more depth and offer examples from coaching conversations.

In these first two chapters, you will also see how the fundamentals of co-active coaching apply to those informal conversations at work and even at home. While it's true that not every conversation we have with another person fits the definition of a co-active conversation opportunity, the awareness of these fundamentals provides insight into those conversations. Sometimes what first appears as a mundane—even trivial—exchange taps into something much more important, deeper, with meaning that wasn't anticipated by either party.

No doubt at some time in your life you've experienced this. The direction of a conversation becomes suddenly more personal, vulnerable perhaps, definitely not planned. By understanding the fundamentals of co-active coaching, you will be better prepared to see the opportunity in these situations and engage more effectively—not as a counselor or problem solver, but in a co-active way that courageously enters the conversation more as a companion on an unexpected journey. In a way, that describes the fundamental nature of every coaching conversation: being present in the moment, open to what shows up, even if we started with a plan.

There is a subtext to every conversation. That subtext is made up of assumptions, expectations, and unspoken agreements. It's also made up of relationship qualities that include individual status, values, and beliefs—all melding together in a conversation that may be about something very ordinary. It's easy to ignore the subtext in favor of focusing on the conversation on the surface; we're more familiar with that option and it's more comfortable, but it can miss the opportunity for a deeper conversation. It is that deeper conversation that builds relationship, trust, and empowered results. An understanding of the co-active model and its fundamentals will help equip you to have more awareness, and it will allow you to bring a wider range of competence to any conversation.

These first two chapters will give you, either as coach or in your leadership role, insight into dimensions of the conversation that are not so visible but have enormous impact on results and the ongoing relationship.

CHAPTER 1

The Co-Active Model

The term *co-active* refers to the fundamental nature of a coaching relationship in which the coach and coachee are active collaborators. In co-active coaching, this is a relationship—in fact an alliance—between two equals for the purpose of meeting the coachee's needs. The term itself brings together the essential human qualities of being and doing:

- Who we are
- Who we are in relationship
- Who we are being and want to be
- How we are actively creating
- What we are doing—or in some cases *not* doing—to achieve the results we want in life and work

Coach and coachee are in this together, "co-operating" as coachees take action.

Four Cornerstones

The four cornerstones represent the fundamental beliefs of a co-active way of being in relationship and conversation at the deepest level. We take a stand for these as essential to the impact that is possible in coaching and any coach-like conversation. The co-active coaching model rests on these four declarations. They form a container that holds the co-active conversation. In fact, the cornerstones make it possible to have a truly co-active conversation. In order for engaged and empowered relationship to exist—the "co" in co-active—and in order for life-giving action on the part of the coachee to manifest, these four create the necessary structure.

People are Naturally Creative, Resourceful, and Whole

We start with this assertion: people are, by their very nature, naturally creative, resourceful, and whole. They are capable: capable of finding answers, capable of choosing, capable of taking action, capable of recovering when things don't go as planned, and, especially, capable of learning. This capacity is wired into all human beings no matter their circumstances. In the co-active model, it is more than a belief; it is a stand we take.

The alternative is a belief that people are fragile and dependent. With that belief, the coach's job would be to guide the coachee to the safest possible outcome. You can feel the difference. When we take a stand for other people's natural creativity and resourcefulness, we become champions on their behalf, not worried hand holders. As coaches, when we assume that others are resourceful and creative, we become curious and open to possibilities. We enter into a process of discovering with the coachee, not dictating. We expect to be amazed.

The key here is *naturally*. Yes, of course there are times when the circumstances feel overwhelming, when even the most resilient human beings feel that the mountain is too high, the road to cross too wide, the effort simply not in their power. Circumstances and that inner sabotaging voice that says "Why bother?" or "You don't have what it takes" can leave anyone feeling much less than creative or resourceful, and just a fraction of whatever whole is. On those days more perhaps than on any others, it is our place as coaches, our gift to see the true, natural selves who were and are still capable. We remind them of their own inner light and help them find it again—because it is there. Naturally.

Focus on the Whole Person

For people who want to be helpful, including most new coaches or people in a coaching role, the question that's often foremost on their minds is "What's the problem to solve?" It's a question that comes from the best of intentions: a desire to understand and provide valuable assistance so that a troublesome problem can be handled quickly and efficiently. There is urgency in the air, and we want to be helpful.

Leaders and managers—even those who truly value coaching as an essential and valuable contribution to their role—still easily fall into this trap. Under enormous pressure to get results and get results *now*, the first task they take on is to identify the problem to be solved. This urge is perfectly understandable, and of course solving problems is important. But leaders manage people, not just problems. Developing talent and creating a more resourceful and effective organization creates sustainable results, long after the presenting problem is solved. Even under organizational stress, this whole-person mind-set sees opportunity not to be overlooked.

When a coach is sitting across from a coachee (even by telephone), the coach is not sitting across from a problem to be solved; the coach is sitting across from a person. This person does have a problem to solve—a change to make, a dream to fulfill, a task to accomplish, a goal to reach. All of that is true. But this person is more than the problem at hand—or the goal, the dream, the task. This is a whole person: heart, mind, body, and spirit. And this issue, whatever it is, is not neatly isolated. It is inexorably entwined in the coachee's whole life.

Maybe the word *focus* is a little misleading. This cornerstone is certainly not a hard, tight, concentrated focus on the whole person. It is more of a soft or broad focus, an attentive focus that includes the whole person and the whole life, listening on many levels. Too often in our eagerness to be helpful we access only the place between our ears. We use the mind to probe and understand and then create logical, pragmatic solutions.

Analysis and logic are worthy and useful attributes, but they are not the whole story. Sometimes a "correct" solution can have emotional consequences that are just as important; sometimes what the mind says yes to, the spirit feels at a loss with. We are not suggesting that a coach should be focusing on coaching heart, mind, body, and spirit as independent elements, but a coach or anyone in a co-active conversation ought to be tuned in to the influences that are present in these different dimensions.

It was not so many years ago that talking about emotions was taboo, especially in the workplace. Today, courses in developing mastery in emotional intelligence are commonplace, thanks to the groundbreaking work of Daniel Goleman. In a similar way, awareness of body language and the exceptional work of somatic practitioners has paved the way to a much better and more widespread conversation about the role of body in communication.

Surely the most sensitive of these dimensions is spirit. *Spirit* is the most elusive term to define, coming by many different names and different expressions, but it is present with every human being. In coaching, *spirit* is not limited to a form of spirituality and certainly not to a religion. But there is a spirit dimension that influences human choices. At the core, it includes the sense of living according to values, or a calling, or a power greater than ourselves. Sometimes it is intuition, a feeling in our gut, and sometimes it is a conviction that we know we must live by. It is a spirit dimension that transcends this one decision; in fact, we only know it is spirit because it feels transcendent.

Obviously, a focus on the whole person also means that as coaches we are aware of all the ways the issue or topic before us is interwoven in this person's life. There is a vast ecology of people and priorities that are interconnected with whatever is the current subject of conversation. It is also entirely possible for the coach and coachee to limit the conversation to a single, narrow subject while at the same time having an antenna for the possibility of connecting this single issue to a broader or deeper conversation. The ability to take the conversation into any area that the coachee finds compelling doesn't mean the coach insists on declaring the destination and going there. Again, the key is increased awareness, because no topic exists in isolation. A decision in one area of life inevitably ripples through all areas of life. An exciting career move may be very fulfilling—and it may affect health, family relationships, free time, and geography. A coach can work effectively with a coachee on a very narrow topic, but in the co-active way there is a larger picture also at play, and that is the whole person.

Dance in This Moment

A conversation is a powerful and dynamic interchange between people. It's natural to pay attention to the content of the conversation—the words, the positions, the ideas—that's often what is most "visible" and easiest to respond to. And yet, as important as the words and content are, there is much more going on in every moment. Every conversation creates tone, mood, nuance. There is as much information, sometimes more in *how* the words are said versus the words chosen; sometimes there is more information in what is *not* said than what is said.

For the coach this becomes an exercise in listening intently at many levels, and of course, choosing when and how to respond, to intervene. The information about what to say or ask does not come from a script. It comes in the moment, in THIS moment, and then the next moment. To "dance in this moment" is to be very present to what is happening right now and respond to that stimulus, not to a master plan.

To "dance" is to respond from a co-active core meaning both "co" as in collaborative, and active, moving the dance forward. In a truly co-active conversation there are moments when the coach leads the dance, moments when the coachee leads the dance, and moments when it is not clear at all who is leading and who is following.

All three states of the dance are natural; the third, the point where it seems to lose leader/follower designation, is a rare state of connection. It is a place of tuned in to each other and a place, frankly, of vulnerability—a willingness, built on extraordinary trust, to go with the flow of the conversation. It does feel like an exquisite dance to the music, both partners in tune with the tempo, tone, and steps. This agility is all for the sake of the coachee's learning and discovery.

Evoke Transformation

Coach and coachee meet in this co-active conversation for a common purpose: the coachee's full life. The topic of the coaching will likely be something quite specific—a fraction of the coachee's life that the coachee is focused on. But if we follow that leaf to the branch and move from the branch to the trunk of the tree and its roots, there is always a deeper connection possible. The goal of the coaching in one session might be clarity and action around a project. The motivation for the coaching could be a new job or promotion, improved fitness, or execution on a business plan. In fact, coachees may have their attention only on the specific goal for that specific topic. The coach, on the other hand, sees the tree and the larger, fully connected life. Coaches in this model hold a vision that sees the topic as an expression of something even more valuable to the coachee. This action at hand is the means to a higher end; it should lead to a life fully lived in whatever area the coachee finds important.

There is a yearning for the very best, the full potential that the coachee can experience. And when that connection ignites between today's goal and life's potential, it is transformative. Now the report, or the job interview, or the 5K race are more than a checked box on a to-do list. They are expressions of inner conviction. The accomplishment is a message about who the coachee can be. There is a shift from the satisfaction of "ahh" to the breakthrough awareness of "aha"—a new strength, a renewed capacity—like finding muscles they didn't know they had or had forgotten they had.

And part of that "aha"—the deeper awareness—is the knowledge that the coachees have an expanded capacity to reach their potential. What they learned from this one experience they naturally apply in others.

This is why we boldly take a stand for evoking transformation as a cornerstone of this co-active model. We see this as a yearning on the part of coaches for all that is possible for coachees, including learning or recovering the inner strength and resourcefulness to evolve, grow, expand from this one area of focus into many avenues of life. Coaches play a key role, by holding a vision of what is possible and by their commitment to transformative experience. Coachees still choose the topic, the action, and the results they want. But by taking a stand for the greatest possible impact from even the smallest action, coaches encourage—and ultimately evoke—transformation.

You don't need to be a professional coach to see how these four cornerstones apply to almost any important conversation. Think about a conversation you recently had at work with a colleague or a conversation you've had with a son or daughter. No doubt you were busy focusing on resolving a particular issue. But think again, with the advantage of hindsight, how the conversation might have turned if you were conscious of the four cornerstones.

How does the quality of the conversation change when you start with a belief that your coworker, son, or daughter is naturally creative, resourceful, and whole? Capable? It's possible the conversation might change from giving advice to being curious: asking more questions and inviting the resourcefulness of that other person. Think about how your awareness shifts when you see the connection between what might seem like ordinary daily business and how this one issue is interconnected with that person's life in ways you probably won't ever know. Those ripples may not be visible in the moment, but they are real.

The ability to dance with whatever shows up is certainly a leadership competency; in today's world of business, great agility is essential. Without necessarily having a name for it, effective leaders display that quality in their work with others every day. Even the fourth cornerstone, "Evoke Transformation," can be a resonant field in which the conversation takes place. That brief conversation has the potential to affirm that colleague, son, or daughter in ways that reverberate long after the presenting issue has been handled.

Of course, this awareness of the depth that is possible by understanding the four cornerstones is not a suggestion that every conversation is meant to be a formal coaching conversation; you will often leave your coach's hat on the rack. Your children, spouse, and employees will be grateful if you do. The central point is to raise your awareness so you can be more effective in any of those roles simply by appreciating the possibilities in any conversation.

The Heart of the Model

From the perspective of a trained coach working with a coachee, we start with a clear commitment: the ongoing relationship between coach and coachee exists only to address the goals of the coachee. So naturally, the coachee's life is the focus at the center of the diagram in figure 1.

There are two ways to think about this. One way is to see the action of the day as part of the big picture for the coachee's life. People make dozens, even hundreds, of decisions every day to do or not do certain things. The choices we make during the day, no matter how trivial they may seem, contribute to creating a life that is more (or less) fulfilling. The decisions we make move us toward or away from better balance in our lives. The choices contribute to a more effective life process or to a process that is less effective. And so at one level, the coachee's action is always wrapped in these three core principles—fulfillment, balance, and process—which we will explore in more depth shortly. They are principles because they are fundamental to the liveliness of life. In the same way that oxygen, fuel, and heat are necessary for fire, these three principles combine to create an ignited life—perhaps "Life" with a capital "L."

The second way is to look at the specific issues the coachee chooses to work with during the coaching sessions. Coachees bring all sorts of agenda items to their coaching. This issue of the day, or week, or month is about life today with an everyday "l" for "life." Yet, whatever the specific issue, there is a way to link it to the larger, more fulfilling Life—a link to Life-giving balance or better process.

Fulfillment

The coachee's definition of fulfillment is always intensely personal. It may include, especially at first, outward measures of success: a great job or promotion, enough money, a certain lifestyle or personal accomplishment. Eventually, the coaching will progress to a deeper definition of fulfillment. It's not about having more. It's not about what fills the coachee's pockets or closets; it's about what fills the coachee's heart and soul.

The Co-Active® Model

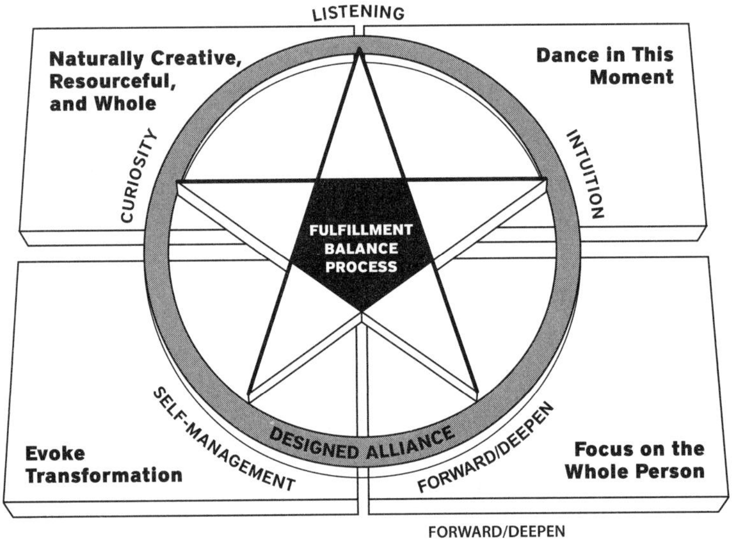

FIGURE 1   The Co-Active Coaching Model

A fulfilling life is a valued life, and coachees will have their own definitions of what they truly value. If they value risk taking, is there enough adventure in their lives? If they value family, are they shortchanging themselves by caving in to the demands of work? What are the personal values they want present in their work? Sorting out values is a way of sorting out life choices, because when the choices reflect the coachee's values, life is more satisfying and often feels effortless. Achieving a certain goal can be very fulfilling—especially as a benchmark—but most coachees find that fulfillment is not the finish line. At its deepest level, fulfillment is about finding and experiencing a life of purpose and service. It is about reaching one's full potential.

Balance

With so many responsibilities and distractions, and at today's high-speed rate of change, balance may feel like an impossible dream. It's especially elusive for most of the people who come to coaching. They tend to be dissatisfied with functioning at some minimum standard of being alive; they want more from life and want to give more back. They can be passionate about the things that matter to them, focused in their commitment, and so intense that sometimes one corner of their lives is a model of excellence while the rest is in ruins. They understand the value of balance and have probably made attempts to achieve it—with good intentions to exercise more, take time off, or reconnect with friends—and found that weeks or months passed without any change. Life is out of balance.

People often seem resigned to being out of balance, as if that's just the way life is. That's the "real world." There's only one way of looking at it, and it looks bad. Coaching for balance, however, focuses on widening the range of perspectives and, therefore, adding more choices. Ultimately, balance is about making choices: saying yes to some things and no to others. This can be challenging. Coachees often want to say yes to more in their lives without making room for it by saying no to something else. This impulse leads to an overwhelmed feeling—and lives that are out of balance.

Balance is a fluid state because life itself is dynamic. Therefore, it makes more sense to look at whether coachees are moving toward balance or away from balance rather than to offer them "balance" as a goal to be achieved. Like the seasons of the year, balance is best viewed over the long haul. It is also a perennial issue, one that coaches will see, in some form or another, many times over in the course of a coaching relationship.

Process

We are always in process. Sometimes it looks frantic; sometimes it looks graceful. Because coaching is effective at achieving results, both coachees and coaches can get drawn into the "results" trap—focusing entirely on the destination and losing sight of the flow of the journey. In fact, process is often compared to a river. As life flows, there will be fast periods of onrushing, white-water progress as well as days of calm, steady currents. But there will also be times of drifting, being stuck in job eddies and relationship whirlpools and backsliding into treacherous swamps. There will be flooding and drought.

The coach's job is to notice, point out, and be with coachees wherever they are in their process. The coach is there to encourage and support, provide companionship around the rocks, and escort coachees through the dark waters as well as to celebrate their skill and success at navigating the difficult passages. Coaching allows coachees to live more fully in a deeper relationship with all aspects of their lives.

Co-active coaching therefore embraces this whole picture of the coachee: fulfillment, balance, and process. These are the core principles at the heart of the coaching model. Together they create the heat and light of a Life that is fully alive.

Designed Alliance for an Empowered Coaching Environment

With the coachee in the center of the co-active coaching model (see figure 1, p. 10), we encircle the coachee and the coachee's agenda; we name this protective circle the designed alliance. In co-active coaching, power is granted to the coaching relationship, not to the coach. Coachee and coach work together to design an effective working relationship that meets the coachee's needs. In fact, coachees play an important role in declaring how they want to be coached. They are involved in creating a powerful relationship that fits their working and learning styles. The relationship is tailored to the communication approach that works best for them. The process of designing the alliance is a model of the mutual responsibility of coachee and coach. Coachees learn that they are in control of the relationship and, ultimately, of the changes they make in their lives.

The Five Contexts

Visually, the coaching model illustrated in figure 1 represents a five-pointed star. Each point of the star is a context that the coach brings to the coaching. Each is a point of contact with the coachee. The coach consistently draws from these contexts in the practice of coaching. In time, and through training, the coach develops these abilities the way a musician develops musical technique. The five contexts are always in play. We present them in one order here in the book, but they are a constellation, not a sequence—essential elements of a complete coaching approach, like five spotlights that are always shining, illuminating the coachee's life.

Listening

Of course, the coach listens to the words that come from the coachee, tracking the content of the coaching conversation. But the most important listening of coaching takes place on a deeper level. It is the listening for the meaning behind the story, for the underlying process, for the theme that will deepen the learning. The coach is listening for the appearance of the coachee's vision, values, and purpose. The coach is also listening for resistance, fear, backtracking, and the voice of the saboteur, who is there to object to change, point out the coachee's shortcomings, and bring up all the reasons why this idea, whatever it is, won't work.

The coach listens at many levels simultaneously to hear where coachees are in their process, to hear where they are out of balance, and to hear their progress on the journey of fulfillment. The coach is listening for the nuance of hesitation, too, for the sour ring of something not quite true. (In chapter 3, we look in depth at three levels of listening.)

Intuition

By listening below the surface, the coach finds the place where the hard data and soft data merge. Intuition is a kind of knowing that resides in the background and is often unspoken. It remains in the background because, for many people, it's not easy to trust. Our culture doesn't validate intuition as a reliable means of drawing conclusions or making decisions, so we hesitate to say what our intuition tells us. We hold back because we don't want to appear foolish. And yet it is one of the most powerful gifts a coach brings to coaching.

As coaches, we receive a great deal of information from the coachee and then, in the moment of coaching, combine it with previous information as well as experience, not only of coaching but also of operating in the world. Add to this one more factor: information that comes from our intuition. We may not call it *intuition*. We may consider it a thought, or a hunch, or a gut feeling. Regardless of how we define it, the impulse emerges from our intuition. For most coaches, intuition is a skill that needs practice and development. It is enormously valuable because, time and again, it synthesizes more impressions and information than we could ever analyze consciously.

Curiosity

One of the fundamental tenets of co-active coaching is that coachees are capable and resourceful and have the answers. The coach's job is to ask the questions, to lead the discovery process. The context of curiosity gives a certain frame to the process of uncovering answers and drawing out insight. Curiosity is open, inviting, spacious, almost playful. And yet it is also enormously powerful. Like scientific curiosity, which explores the deepest questions of matter, life, and the universe, curiosity in coaching allows coach and coachee to enter the deepest areas of the coachee's life, side by side, simply looking, curious about what they will find.

Because the coach is not an inquisitor but is really on the coachee's side in this exploration, the coach can ask powerful questions that break through old defenses. When coachees learn to be curious about their lives, it reduces some of the pressure and lowers the risk. They become more willing to look in the dark places and try the hard things because they are curious, too.

Forward and Deepen

The two products of the work the coachee and coach do together—action and learning—combine to create change. Because the notion of action that moves the coachee forward is so central to the purpose of coaching, we often say that one of the purposes of coaching is to "forward the action" of the coachee.

The other force at work in the human change process is learning. Learning is not simply a byproduct of action; it is an equal and complementary force. Learning generates new resourcefulness, expanded possibilities, and stronger muscles for change.

One of the common misunderstandings about coaching is that it is simply about getting things done: performing at a higher level. Because of this misunderstanding, coaching has been compared to hiring a nagging parent who will make sure your bed is made and your homework is done. In some organizations, it's the image of a schoolteacher with a ruler, poised to measure your failure and provide the punishment. But coaching is not just about getting things done; it is just as importantly about continuing to learn, especially to learn how the action is or is not contributing to the core principles. This connection between action and learning and the core principles is key. Gandhi is quoted as saying, "There is more to life than increasing its speed." In the same way, there is more to life, at least in the co-active model, than increasing action.

Self-Management

In order to truly hold the coachee's agenda, the coach must get out of the way—not always an easy thing to do. Self-management is the coach's ability to set aside personal opinions, preferences, pride, defensiveness, and ego. The coach needs to be "over there" with the coachee, immersed in the coachee's situation and struggle, not "over here," dealing with the coach's own thoughts, analysis, and judgments. Self-management means giving up the need to look good and be right; the light should be shining on the coachee, not the coach. Self-management is about awareness of impact. In the course of a coaching relationship, coachees also learn about self-management in their own lives. They experience the modeling and develop their own awareness of impact insight.

The Coach's Role in the Model

The coach is a kind of change agent, entering the equation for change without knowing what the outcome will be. Goals and plans, new practices, new benchmarks, and achievements of every kind are all part of the coachee's ongoing work, facilitated by the coaching interaction. The coach is a catalyst, an important element in the process of accelerating change.

This is more than a passive role. We see coaching, especially the form presented here, as a role of service that requires commitment and presence on the part of the coach. Whether the coach is working with individual private coachees or has been hired to work with coachees inside an organization, a sense of purpose, even a higher purpose, is definitely an underlying element. In the world of co-active coaching, we would say that coaching exists to serve the coachee's higher purpose. When we aim for this higher purpose, we create the means for transformative change in coachees and, by extension, in families and organizations. The ripples of change in a coachee's higher purpose move out into the world.

To be present there, in that conversation, contributing to that change is enormously gratifying. It fulfills a sense of higher purpose in the coach's life. Making a difference—helping others to achieve their dreams and reach their potential—this is why coaches are drawn to this work.

The Co-Active Way: A Broader Application of the Model

While we have presented the co-active coaching model from the perspective of the trained coach in an intentionally designed coaching relationship, we have also described a broader application that applies to informal conversations that benefit enormously from the deeper awareness an understanding of co-active coaching brings. As a manager working with an employee about a pressing issue at hand, you are not likely to have your attention on that person's fulfilling life, life balance, or process in any specific sense. Yet, at some level, your leadership intelligence will recognize those principles in the background even if your attention is on the details in the foreground. The most effective leaders see a whole person with potential, and they view the issue in the moment as an opportunity for development. The skills and awareness that you develop through this practice have the power to help you create new levels of empowered and effective relationships.

CHAPTER 2

The Co-Active Coaching Relationship

Coaching is not so much a methodology as it is a relationship, a particular kind of relationship. Yes, there are skills to learn and a wide variety of tools available, but the real art of effective coaching comes from the coach's ability to work within the context of relationship. That's true for the professional coach in a structured coaching relationship, and it's just as true for the manager having a coaching conversation with a direct report. There will be significant differences in the form and circumstances of the conversation, but all coaching takes place in the context of intentional relationship.

Let's begin this topic of co-active relationship with how that looks for the professional coach. It starts with an awareness that every coachee is in a unique life and work situation, with unique goals and desire for change, unique abilities, unique interests, and even unique habits of self-sabotage. We can talk in very general terms about focus areas that coachees often pursue—career change, life transition, performance improvement, leadership in the workplace, health and wellness issues—but only in the broadest terms.

Add to this picture the fact that goals change over time as coachees clarify what is important, as they dig deeper into what motivates them, and as they take action and learn from the action they take. There is no "authorized universal coaching reference guide" with standardized diagnoses and coaching solutions neatly defined. Coaching is inherently dynamic; that is one of the fundamental qualities of coaching and a reason for its power as a medium for change. Coaching is personal; coaching creates a unique, empowered relationship for change.

In co-active coaching, we also emphasize the peer relationship: that coach and coachee have equal, though different, roles. They are co-active in the relationship, so they are collaborators, working together for the benefit of the coachee.

We can picture this relationship as a triangle (see figure 2: The Coaching Power Triangle). The coach grants power to the coaching relationship. The coachee also grants power to the relationship, not to the coach. Coachees are in turn empowered by the relationship—empowered to take charge of their lives and the choices they make. In this figure, all the power of the relationship exists to serve the coachee. In fact, the co-active coach must make the shift from "I am powerful" to "the coaching relationship

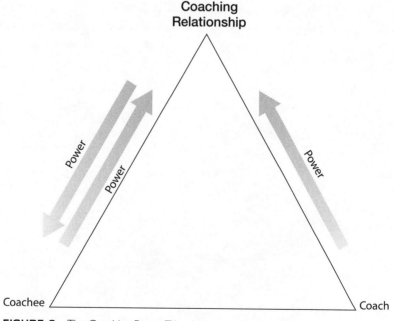

FIGURE 2 The Coaching Power Triangle

is powerful." Powerful coaching is not about being a powerful coach; it is about the power the coachee experiences.

You can think of the coaching relationship as a recharging station where coachees tap into the source of energy they need in order to get over the hurdles in their lives. They can't get the work done if the energy level is low. The power comes not directly from the coach, however, but from the relationship—the synergy of energy coachees bring in the form of desire and motivation, and the energy coaches bring in the form of their commitment, skills, and understanding of human change.

This energy and empowerment model takes on a third dimension when we shift to co-active coaching in the context of an informal—but still intentional—coaching relationship for team leaders, managers, and supervisors. (See figure 3: The Coaching Culture Pyramid.) Looking from the side at this model, the role of leader as coach and coachee are still visible; the important role of the organization is hidden but still provides essential structure and support, in this case, to both the leader and the coachee.

In this three-dimensional view of coaching in organizations, each of the three dimensions benefits. There is a solid base of empowerment that extends to coachee, coach, and ultimately the organization. In a coaching culture, the organization, the coach, and the coachee all grant power to

FIGURE 3   The Coaching Culture Pyramid

the relationships. When the dynamics of the relationship are empowered, coachee and coach both grow. As they grow, their capacity and ability to contribute also grows. The energy flows in three dimensions from this self-charging base of power built on a coaching commitment and what that gives relationships. It is also an image that reinforces the essential importance of the unique contributions of each role to the whole. In this case, the synergy is three-dimensional.

The Coaching Environment

At its most fundamental, a coaching interaction is a conversation between a coach and another person or—in team or relationship coaching—a coach and two or more people. But this is no ordinary, everyday conversation. An effective coaching conversation has a clear and powerful mandate that is about learning, change, and growth. This is about evoking transformation as we describe it in the four cornerstones. The presenting topic, the consideration of action, and the commitment and accountability that result are all part of the larger purpose. The environment in which the conversation takes place is crucial.

By *environment*, we mean both a physical environment and a relationship environment that is made up of ground rules, an understanding of expectations, and mutual agreements that support the coaching process. Most conversations take place in noisy environments—and that noise is more than the audible, high-decibel, cacophony in a busy environment. It includes distractions, priorities, emotions, deadlines, family matters . . . the list of noisemakers is endless. The goal for an effective coaching conversation is a relationship environment that is as clear and as quiet as possible, devoid of as much noise as can be eliminated.

In co-active coaching, we talk about two core characteristics of an effective coaching environment:

1. It is safe enough for coachees to take the risks they need to take.
2. It is a courageous place where coachees are able to approach their lives and the choices they make with motivation, creativity, and commitment.

By the way, *safe* does not necessarily mean *comfortable*. Significant change may be highly uncomfortable, and yet there are ways to ensure that the experience is safe. Like the rock climber ascending the cliff face, striving for the summit, coachees may find the process exhilarating, exhausting, and scary. But knowing that there is the equivalent of a belay team holding their rope and ensuring their safety gives them the confidence to keep climbing.

Certain qualities characterize an environment that is safe and courageous for coachees. When those conditions are in place, coachees are able to reach higher and go further because the trust and assurance that is built into the relationship is *more* than a safety net. It is a dynamic springboard of support that allows individuals to reach for what otherwise might seem unreachable. These essential environmental qualities give shape to what we have called the *container* for the coaching relationship.

Confidentiality

Making change means disturbing the familiar and well-established order of things. It may be deeply satisfying, even exciting to embark on that change, and yet it may still feel risky. Even if the coachee and the coachee's wider world of connections are completely committed to and supportive of the change, change by its nature is an unknown. If coachees are going to risk making significant change, they must be able to risk talking freely with their coach. Courageous disclosure is crucial because it leads to the discovery that is necessary for action. Without the safety and reassurance that confidentiality provides, the coaching will be tentative, and there will always be an undercurrent of wonder about what is possibly being withheld.

Coaches who work with coachees inside organizations have to deal with a more complex environment. Confidentiality between coach and coachee is still a key condition for safe and courageous conversation, but because the organization has a vested interest in the result, it usually requires some form of reporting on the coaching. Typically, it is the coachee who is the one who takes responsibility for reporting the nature of the coaching work; this allows the coachee to disclose what is most relevant to the organization while preserving confidentiality between the coachee and the coach.

Trust

An agreement to hold the coaching conversation confidential is one key component in building trust. Trust is also built over time as both coachee and coach learn they can be counted on and the coachee learns that the relationship delivers results. Trust is built from small things like being punctual for coaching sessions and from a pattern of reliability. Because trust works both ways, it is as important for the coach as it is for the coachee. Coaches must be trustworthy in their actions.

Relationship is also built and trust expanded by coaches simply believing in their coachees. We live in a culture that, for the most part, demands that people prove themselves and demonstrate their worthiness by performing to some standard before they are accepted into the circle. The culture creates relationships in which the emphasis is on proving, explaining, and justifying. A coaching relationship built on the premise that coachees are naturally creative, resourceful, and whole and are capable of making the best choices is a relationship founded on basic trust in the coachee's capacity and integrity. Coachees see that they have a person in their lives who believes they can do what they say they can do, who believes they can be the people they say they want to be.

It is a paradox that coaches believe completely in their coachees and, at the same time, rigorously hold them accountable. But by *accountable* we do not mean a context of judgment, as in "prove it to me." Rather, as coaches we are simply asking coachees to account for their promise of action and the insight of learning. We ask, "How did it go?" and, "What did you learn?" Coachees see that the coach is really on their side, respecting their vision and their action plans but also willing to be honest and direct for their sake.

By creating a courageous container, coaches ensure that coachees feel safe enough to take risks, in fact to be vulnerable. With each act of vulnerability there is a little more breathing room built; a little more trust is added to the relationship. That additional trust makes the environment safer and allows coachees to be more courageous. When the environment is right, it creates its own self-reinforcing system for vulnerability and growth.

Speaking the Truth

We could also call this attribute of a coaching environment "getting real." A safe and courageous space for change must be, by definition, a place where the truth can be told. It is a place where coachees can tell the whole truth about what they have done, and not done, without becoming a worrying child to the coach as parent. The coaching environment is a place without judgment. It is a place where the coach expects the truth from the coachee because truth carries no consequence other than learning, discovery, and new insight.

Coachees expect the truth from the coach because that is the inherent promise in the coaching relationship. Coachees are often so close to their own situations, so wrapped up in their own histories and habitual patterns, that they are sometimes unable to see the truth accurately. This may be one of their reasons to seek out coaching. They rely on the coach for the acuity that sees through the chaos and fog. This should be one relationship in which coachees can count on straightforward and honest interactions.

Truth telling doesn't have to be confrontational, although it may confront. It can be handled with sharpness or softness, but it confronts the usual tacit acceptance of the coachee's explanations (or excuses). Truth telling refuses to sidestep or overlook: it boldly points out when the emperor is not wearing clothes. There is no inherent judgment in telling the truth. Coaches are merely stating what they see. Withholding the truth serves neither the coachee nor the coaching relationship.

A real relationship is not built on being nice; it's built on being real. Coaches can be careful . . . or they can care *fully* and commit to telling the truth as they see it. When the coach has the courage to tell the truth, the coachee gets a model of the art of being straight; in the process, more trust is built between coach and coachee.

Openness and Spaciousness

One of the qualities that make the coaching relationship work is spaciousness. This is a place where coachees can breathe, experiment, fantasize, and strategize without limitation. It is another world, a place of wide-eyed dreams. It is a space in which they can vent their anger, troubles, spite, perceptions of injustice, and regrets. It is a place where failure is acknowledged as a means for learning, where curiosity and creativity replace rigid rules and historical absolutes.

For the coach, spaciousness also means complete detachment from any particular course of action or any results that coachees achieve. Coaches continue to care about their coachees (e.g., their agendas, their health, and their growth) but not the road they take to get there, the speed of travel, or the detours they might make along the way—as long as they continue to move toward the results they want. Ultimately, coaching is not about what the coach delivers but about what coachees create. A coach may propose a course of action to get the results a coachee desires. That is fine. Brainstorming is part of coaching and can make a valuable contribution to the coachee's process. But in order to preserve openness in the relationship, coaches must not be attached to whether coachees take their suggestions. The spaciousness of the relationship requires that coachees have many channels open to creative inspiration and not be restricted to the coach's good ideas, no matter how sound or grounded in experience. In this way, coachees are able to explore the widest range of possibilities.

The Designed Alliance

So far we've been talking about this relationship between coachee and coach as if it were conceptual. Actually, we believe it is important for coachee and coach to consciously and deliberately design their working relationship and continue to redesign it as necessary up through and including its completion of their work together. The designed alliance surrounds the coach and coachee in the co-active coaching model (see figure 1, p. 10) and represents the container within which coach and coachee do their work.

The form of the design will be different for different coaches and unique to each coach-coachee relationship. The conversation that creates the design focuses on the assumptions and expectations of coach and coachee. The purpose of this intentional conversation is to clarify the process and expected outcomes and provide a forum for negotiating the design of a relationship that is as powerful as possible for both coachee and coach.

In simplest terms, the design of the alliance looks at questions such as *What are the conditions that need to be in place for the two of us to work together effectively? What are the obstacles or potential obstacles? What fundamental questions need to be answered in order to get the most out of this process?* And as the coaching continues, there will be ongoing questions: *What is working and what is not? What do we need to change in order to make the coaching relationship more effective or have more impact?*

This first conversation about consciously creating an effective working relationship is just the beginning. Continuing to be open, to find new or more effective ways of working together, is an ongoing part of a co-active coaching relationship. In one way, the strength of a coachee's ability to make changes in his or her work and life is a measure of the strength in the coach-coachee relationship. And the strength of that relationship is measured by the commitment to an open, fearless, and continuous design of their alliance over time.

For leaders, managers, and supervisors, the "design" of the alliance will not be as structured, but the essence of the alliance is still important. It is certainly *not* "doing coaching" on team members or direct reports. The context for coaching in an informal organizational or leadership situation is a commitment to support and development. This commitment to development is the essence of the business case for coaching as a leadership and management competency. As a team leader you may not have a private, one-hour alignment and design of the alliance conversation with every team member. But coaching flourishes best in a culture where a coaching conversation is commonly practiced and understood for its contribution to helping everyone be more successful.

Coaching Format

Over the past decade, coaching as a practice and as a profession has taken root in a myriad of forms, and the variety of environments in which we find coaching and coaching skills being used continues to expand. Today you will find co-active coaches working from home offices and inside institutions and organizations. You will find co-active coaches coaching in prisons, hospitals, and corporate boardrooms. Some coaches work as employees within organizations, often with other job duties in addition to coaching. Others combine coaching with consulting work in order to provide ongoing implementation support and follow-up.

Many coaches work with private, individual coachees. Some specialize in working with teams or people in relationship. Coaching today is global and cross-cultural. Coaches and coachees cover dozens of demographic categories: age, income, education, ethnic background, and job position. Many coaches specialize in a select interest or career area and focus on working with CEOs, immigrants or expatriates, artists and musicians, or parents and their teenagers.

The environment within which coaching takes places is equally varied. Many coaches work with coachees by telephone, with regularly scheduled, often weekly, appointments, although there are many variations. Some coaches and coachees prefer in-person coaching, whether at the coachee's site, at the coach's office, or off-site. Coaches may contract with coachees for a fixed period of time, such as three months, six months, or a year. Other coaches establish ongoing, open-ended relationships with coachees. Coaching takes place in paneled boardrooms, inner-city homes, and mountain retreats.

Within that framework, coaches bring their coaching training and experience and a wide variety of tools and means of assessment. The permutations of forms and environments continue, inspired by the imagination of coaches and the interests of coachees. And yet, no matter what form the coaching takes, we believe that it will be most effective when coach and coachee create a safe and courageous space for the work, when they construct a shared understanding and alignment on the purpose and value of coaching, and, especially, when they consciously design their working alliance.

Getting Started

Coaches typically begin a working relationship with an initial process that is part coachee orientation and part self-discovery work for coachees. This foundation-setting process familiarizes coachees with the coaching process, provides an opportunity to design the alliance, and begins the work of clarifying coachee issues and goals. There is no standardized form for this. With some coaches, it is a brief interview or a page or two of basic questions, all handled in the initial coaching session. Other coaches might use several sessions, assessments of various kinds, and interviews with the coachee's coworkers, direct reports, or family members. Alternately, this discovery process might be done as visioning work at an off-site location.

In this initial work, coachees learn what to expect from coaching. It is also a time for them to clarify where they are, where they're headed, the strengths they will use to get there, and the obstacles that often interfere.

The coach typically covers these four areas:

- Logistics
- You are here. Where is here?
- Designing the future
- Orientation to coaching

Logistics

One of the first, obvious elements in getting started is communication and agreement on fundamental ground rules and administrative procedures. Settling such details as appointment schedules, cancellation policy, and payment arrangements (when appropriate) is part of getting under way, but it is also key in creating relationship. Coachees will begin to set expectations of their coach and the coaching process based on the coach's handling of these administrative procedures. How coaches handle the details, especially in the area of getting agreement, sets a tone and creates a particular environment.

You Are Here. Where Is Here?

This discovery phase focuses on where coachees are today and how they got there. It's a conversation about where they are and the issues at hand, what is at stake, what moves them, what blocks them. The conversation might address such issues as life purpose or mission, values, principles, or personal beliefs. Often, the coach will make an overall assessment of satisfaction in the significant areas of the coachee's life using a tool like the Wheel of Life (see figure 4) or a version of the wheel created specifically for a coachee's situation. (See the Co-Active Online Toolkit [*coactive.com/toolkit*] for more information on using this and other tools for discovery.)

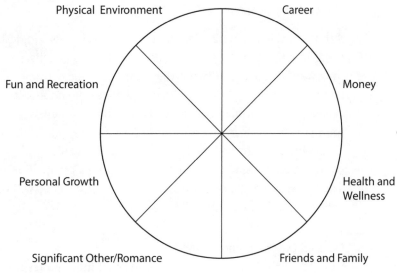

FIGURE 4   The Wheel of Life

Coachees and coach might talk about previous disappointments and successes in order to get an idea of what does and doesn't work, where coachees are fulfilled, and the strategies they use to handle obstacles and derailment. In this phase, coachee and coach are beginning the process of really getting to know this person, the coachee, from the inside out: the bright places, the dark places, the effective places, and the not-so-effective places.

The coach may use assessment tools or exercises, but at the heart of the discovery process are answers to simple, powerful questions: *Where do you want to make a difference in your life? What do you value most in your relationship with others? What works for you when you are successful at making changes? Where do you usually get stuck? What motivates you? How do you deal with disappointment or failure? How are you about doing what you say you'll do?*

The answers also point very clearly to the design of the most effective coaching relationship. For example, the question *Where do you usually get stuck?* leads to a logical next question, *How would you like me to respond as your coach when you're stuck?* In that exchange, coachees experience and contribute to the design of the alliance.

Designing the Future

A third area of this initial work involves the outcomes and desires coachees bring to coaching. Here the focus is on having coachees describe what they want to change or what they want to achieve. Most coachees have one or two primary areas of focus. Chances of success are better when coachees concentrate on one or two key points of change, so part of the foundation-setting conversation is designed to clarify those key areas. These future outcomes will be the result of achieving goals, fulfilling commitments, changing habits, and bringing a compelling vision to life. The initial conversation also explores who the coachee will be in order to create that new future.

Desired Outcome and Goals

Coachees bring a desire for change to coaching. The results they have in mind may be vaguely defined or crystal clear, but in either case, coachees have not yet been able to achieve the results they want. Desired outcomes may be as specific as a particular goal, or coachees may want to move toward a certain state of being, such as "balanced," "living well with a life-threatening illness," or "more fulfilled with my work."

Part of the initial process will be devoted to clarifying outcomes and, in many cases, refining broadly stated desires into specific goals: What will happen? By when? And how will coachees know they have achieved the results they want? Coach and coachee work together to clarify the goals as well as develop strategies for achieving them. Just as important to achieving results is putting new practices in place. Eliminating life-draining habits while implementing sustaining, life-giving practices is another important focus of the coaching process.

Compelling Vision

We can be pushed down the road by deadlines and expectations and to-do lists. We can be driven by the desire for money or accomplishment or by the promises we make. Or we can be pulled down the road by the gravitational force of a compelling vision, like water running downhill. You can feel the difference between these two forces: pushed or driven on one hand, or pulled irresistibly on the other. Discovering what draws us has the power to overcome the bonds of lethargy and fear. Finding the compelling vision can take any goal, action, or outcome and invest it with new power. An important element in the initial discovery work with coachees is uncovering or igniting this vision.

Who You Need to Be

The classic definition of *crazy* is to continue to do things the same way and expect different results. The truth is, if nothing changes, nothing changes. Very often, something new on the outside, like a new outcome, includes the creation of something new on the inside. In order to achieve the results they want, coachees very likely will need to change attitudes, paradigms, or underlying beliefs. The beginning of a new coaching relationship is an ideal time to peel back the accumulated layers of identity and old roles to uncover the authentic person within.

Orientation to Coaching

Another outcome for the foundation-setting process is to orient the coachee to coaching. Even coachees who have worked with a coach before could use the opportunity to talk through assumptions and concerns and openly share expectations of coaching and each other. In this way both coach and coachee take a stand on behalf of the coaching relationship. A clear, forthright conversation helps reinforce frank, unrestrained, and hence co-active groundwork.

Homeostasis

Part of the orientation to coaching ought to include a few words about homeostasis, a natural, often subconscious resistance to change. "Old habits die hard," as the saying goes. So do old beliefs and old ways of relating to others. Particularly in the middle of change, when the old way is undone and the new way is not yet embedded, there is a strong pull back to the familiar, the known, even if it didn't get coachees the results they wanted.

Change requires the expenditure of energy, and continuing the process of change requires sustaining energy. Some change will be easy; other change will not be so easy. There will often be a tendency, or a temptation at least, to backslide. It's better for coachees to be aware and prepared, so that if the temptation appears, it does not feel like they are failing. Homeostasis, the natural tendency to keep things just as they are, is also inherent in the system.

Every individual, whether a private coachee or an organizational coachee, lives within a system, and the system itself often contributes to the resistance to change. Those surrounding the coachee may not want change; perhaps they weren't consulted about it and yet will be affected. Again, an awareness of the system's gripping power to hold on to things the way they are can help coachees as they move through changes.

The Neuroscience of Coaching

The impact of coaching shows up in change—that's the clearest evidence that coaching works. We see new behavior. To the outward and visible change, over the last few years there has been a growing understanding of what happens internally in mind-set, attitude and process that supports change in a coaching relationship. There is solid science behind why coaching works.

Coaching activates the imagination and enlists the power of curiosity. The neuroscience research reinforces what coaches have known from experience: where the attention goes, energy flows. And that energy is generative. It actually creates new neural pathways—new attitudes, new beliefs, new expectations, and, over time, new results that are sustainable because they are built on those neural pathways.

Coaching creates bonding, deepening trust and commitment through relationship. Coachees are empowered by that interaction—especially in the co-active way because it is designed to be an empowering relationship for change. The brain chemistry reinforces the impact that caring relationship creates.

Neuroscience examines the interrelationship between the two hemispheres of the brain—the interaction of creativity and cognition—both are necessary for an effective coaching outcome: a combination of clear plans and proactive imagination. Transformative coaching is the natural, very human result of thoughtful consideration and emotional stirring and commitment.

There is much more to the science than we have room for here, but it is a fascinating and emerging field that confirms experience and provides insight into the power of change.[1]

The Bigger Picture

In order for coaching to work, there must be commitment on the part of the coachee to exploring, changing, learning, taking risks, persevering even when it is difficult, and investing the time and energy. Coachees must be willing to go beyond their comfort zones and step into the unknown for the sake of change. Without this commitment, coaching drifts and devolves into chitchat or to-do lists that often don't get done. Fortunately, most coachees are energized and willing when they start. This is the perfect time for coachees to clarify and declare their commitment.

Coaches, in turn, need to be clear about their commitment to their coachees. It is a commitment to dig deeply and courageously, to listen intently to the words spoken and those unspoken. Coaching with this level of commitment can be exciting and inspiring. It will not be trivial. The coach who is committed to coachees and their ultimate goals is willing to challenge, incite, motivate, encourage, and sometimes insist that coachees take charge. This is the cornerstone of evoking transformation in action.

When coaches bring 100 percent of their effort and expertise and match the coachee's commitment with their own, it makes theirs a truly co-active relationship. This mutual commitment and the designed alliance between coachee and coach create the safe and courageous space in which coachees can do the important work of their lives.

A Co-Active Way for Leaders

As we said at the beginning of this chapter, the coaching form will look different if you are practicing coaching concepts and tools as a team leader, manager, or supervisor. The form of the relationship will be less structured and more informal. The topic of the coaching conversation will arise naturally from the business and work at hand. The subject will

---

[1] For more information about neuroscience and coaching, check out these sites: *beaboveleadership* *.com* and *neuroscienceforcoaches.com.*

still be very important, but it will more likely be focused on short-term outcomes than on long-term personal goals.

There is a clear business purpose for coaching. It goes way beyond resolving the presenting issue, and it includes the development of employees, particularly leaders, managers, and supervisors. Each coaching conversation, whether formal or informal, benefits both coachee and coach, and as we saw in the pyramid (figure 3), it benefits the organization as well.

In fact, in an organizational setting, the ultimate benefit is the creation of a co-active culture that permeates and empowers all relationships. Not every conversation is an opportunity to coach, but every conversation is an opportunity to experience the power of being held in a co-active relationship. The culture becomes an environment that is safe and courageous—a container where there is a clear expectation of openness, trust, and support for all people to reach higher.

There is a way to create that culture and to engage in powerful coaching interaction for coach and coachee. In part 2 we provide the contexts that define the co-active way in action. In the next five chapters, we address the question *How do we do that?*

PART 2

Co-Active Contexts

So far we have looked at the coaching conversation through the lens of the co-active model, and we have described what distinguishes a co-active relationship as it applies to coaching or to leaders and managers in a coaching role. In this section we describe what distinguishes that role: what the trained coach, leader, or manager brings to the co-active conversation. These are the five co-active contexts:

- Listening
- Intuition
- Curiosity
- Forward and Deepen
- Self-Management

Each of the five is a competency that the coach (or leader or manager in a co-active leadership conversation) brings to the interaction. Imagine a coachee standing in a spot that is surrounded by five lights. One of the lights might be brighter than the others at this moment, but all five are switched on. Each one of the lights represents a particular competency that is essential to an effective co-active conversation. In the flow of the conversation, the coach uses instinct and training to draw on one of the five competencies. With experience and practice, coaches can hone these five competencies into effective tools for empowering conversation.

There are skills associated with each of the competencies, and in each of the following chapters we will describe those skills and give examples. The skills are the visible methods for bringing these five contexts to life in the moment. They are the action associated with the ability described by the context. Each of the chapters also contains sample coaching conversations that illustrate the skills, as well as suggested exercises you can use to develop the skills.

CHAPTER 3

Listening

To be truly listened to is a striking experience, partly because it is so rare. When another person is totally with you—leaning in, interested in every word, eager to empathize—you feel seen and understood. People open up when they know they're really being listened to; they expand, they have more presence. They feel safer and more secure as well, and trust grows. A true commitment to listening well is important in any conversation, but it is especially critical to effective coaching, which is why it is the first of the five contexts we discuss.

Listening is a talent each of us is given in some measure. People who become coaches tend to be gifted listeners to begin with. But listening is also a skill that people can learn and develop through training and practice. Masterful coaches have taken their abundant gift and brought it to a high level of proficiency. Indeed, they use it with the same unconscious grace an athlete uses in a sport or a musician in a performance.

Most people do not listen at a very deep level. With the pressure and pace of their everyday occupations and preoccupations, they survive by just getting by. Conversations skim along the surface. Social media have trained us to "converse" in 140-character bites. Pressing the *like* button has replaced even that. Who has time for anything deeper? On one level it's entirely understandable, but it's a little like living on fast food. It misses the opportunity for a satisfying and nutritious meal. A one-on-one coaching session is a time set aside for a deeper, more fulfilling conversation, and for coaches, listening in new ways is key. For leaders and managers, the conversation is likely to be briefer—not the whole buffet—but even a short coach-like conversation has the ability to nourish the relationship and feed the other person along the way.

In everyday listening, we listen mostly to the words. The focus is on what you said and what I said. Think of all the arguments in which the crux of the fight was the precise words that were used: "That's not what you said." "It's what I meant." "But it's not what you said." Team leaders and team members often engage in conversations on a superficial—but often important—level where the pressure is on to state the problem, evaluate the options, choose a solution, and move on as rapidly as possible. Sometimes that's all that's needed. However, if it's the only form of conversation that happens, then in the linear race to the finish line huge opportunities for creative exploration and collaboration—the opening for constructive consideration and harvesting the learning—are lost.

Another common occurrence in life and organizations is how tenuous the actual connection is in conversations. We start a conversation, but within seconds we've disconnected to process the words internally or to pay attention to one of a hundred other distractions—whether they are also important, just attractive, or simply nagging. We live in a mostly wireless world where we connect and disconnect instantly and invisibly, and the same things happen in conversation.

Maybe you've noticed this in yourself or in others. Instead of really listening, we start thinking about what we'll say next. We look for a comparable story—or one that's just a little more dramatic: "You think that was scary? Let me tell you about the time I . . . " We get caught up in our own feelings, we take things personally, we listen at a superficial level as we evaluate and judge what the other person is saying.

The absence of real listening is especially prevalent at work. Under pressure to get the job done, we listen for the minimum of what we need to know so we can move on to the next fire that needs fighting. The consequence? It's no wonder people feel like mere functions in a whirling machine, not human beings. It's no wonder that "employee engagement" is a serious issue in organizations today. Everybody's talking; nobody's listening.

Effective coaching—whether you are a trained coach or this employee's manager—requires effective listening that is both attuned and adept. The best listeners know how to maximize the listening interaction. *Interaction* is the right word, too, because listening is not simply passively hearing. There is action in listening.

Awareness and Impact

There are two aspects of listening in a co-active context. One is awareness; the other is impact.

Awareness includes the information we receive in what we hear with our ears, of course, but we also listen with all of our senses and with our intuition. We hear, see, and experience sounds, words, images, feelings, and energy. We are attentive to all the information we draw in from our senses. We are multifaceted receivers with many receptors of various kinds, all of which are taking in information. We notice the pace of the delivery, the pitch and tone, the modulation of the voice. We sense the pressure behind the words—the voice might be soft or hard edged, tentative or enraged. We listen not only to the person but, simultaneously, to everything else that is happening in the environment.

When we're together in person or in a videoconference setting, we can observe body language as part of the communication. Over the phone, we sense emotion, and the silence is often filled with revealing information. Since we can't halt the flow to analyze, discern, and interpret meaning from all the incoming sources, the key is to stay open, be aware, and remain receptive.

The second aspect, impact, points to the effect of our listening on others—specifically, the impact of the coach's listening on the coachee. To be an effective listener, you need to be conscious not only of what you are listening to, but also of the impact you have when you act on your awareness. Most of the time, this consciousness occurs just below the surface while your attention is still on the other person.

Imagine you're in a fencing match. All of your attention is focused on the opponent as you instantaneously make choices and respond, parry, and thrust. Your attention is not on the choices you are making; that would break your concentration, with possibly disastrous results. Once the match is over, you can recap the action and review the choices you made. Similarly, when you listen with awareness of your impact, you are not thinking about what you take in or what you're going to do with your awareness. Your listening is hyperconscious and subconscious at the same time.

What you do with your awareness, the choices you make, will have an impact. For example, imagine you're in a crowded room and you smell smoke. There might be a fire. Your attention is drawn to the smoke. You notice it. That's the first aspect of the awareness. Then you decide what to do with this information. You might yell "Fire!" or you might mention it casually to the host. You could grab a fire extinguisher and shoulder your way through the crowd to heroically fight the blaze, or you might slip quietly out the side door. Each of these choices will have a different impact. There will be different consequences depending on what you do with your awareness.

Clearly, listening is not passive, especially in the coaching relationship. In our listening model, we describe three levels of listening. These three levels give the coach an enormous range and, ultimately, the ability to listen at a very deep level.

Level I: Internal Listening

At Level I, our awareness is on ourselves. We listen to the words of the other person, but our attention is on what it means to us personally. At Level I, it's all about "me": my thoughts, my judgments, my feelings, my conclusions about myself and others. Whatever is happening with the other person is coming back to us through a diode: a one-way energy trap that lets information in but not out. We're absorbing information by listening, but we are holding it in a trap that recycles it. At Level I, there is only one question: *What does this mean to me?*

There are times certainly when listening at this level is entirely appropriate. For example: Traveling alone to a new city, you are likely to be operating at Level I most of the time. On your way to the airport you're thinking about where to check in, how long the security lines will be, whether you remembered your passport, how much time is left before the flight, and whether or not you will be able to bring food onboard. For the rest of the trip, in fact, you are likely to be listening mostly to your own thoughts and needs. All of your attention is on yourself, as it should be.

Another indication that you are operating at Level I is a strong desire for more information. You want answers, explanations, details, and data. The internal conversation might sound like this: *The flight is delayed? But*

I'll be late. When will we leave? How can I let people know I might be delayed? Is there another flight? Did I bring enough to read? The purpose of information gathering at Level I is to meet your own needs.

Another typical setting for Level I is a restaurant. Your awareness is self-directed, and the impact of Level I listening is all about you. The consequences affect your pleasure, your health, your satisfaction, and your wallet: *Do I want a beverage before ordering? What are the specials today? Is the chair comfortable? Is there a draft? Am I too close to the kitchen? How are the prices? Can I afford it?* You are conscious of your thoughts and feelings.

The decisions, choices, and judgments you make are all about you. You love certain kinds of fish—but not if they serve the whole fish with those dead blank eyes staring up from the plate. You think about the weight you want to lose, so you decide to order the low-fat dressing on the side. Your internal mind chatter is at maximum here. Even though you might be sitting across the table from someone you are madly in love with, your awareness is entirely at Level I until you have ordered.

Level 1 also includes listening to all the echoes in your own mind. In the midst of an important conversation with a colleague about an upcoming project deadline, you might find yourself thinking, *I wonder what's for lunch. I should have worn a warmer coat this morning. I must remember to check my credit card balance. Who's that new person in marketing?*

Another easy trap for leaders and managers that results in listening at Level 1 is the strong, trained, and rewarded drive to solve problems—as quickly as possible. The possibilities for a cocreated, collaborative solution vanish as the leader or manager listens only to his or her own thoughts, analysis, and opinions about what's best, in a compelling drive to answer the question.

Level I informs us about ourselves and what's going on around us. It's also where we figure things out and understand. It's very important. Coachees need to be at Level I. That's their job: to look at themselves and their lives—to process, think about, feel, understand. But it is definitely not appropriate for the coach to be operating at this self-absorbed level for any length of time. Coaches, being human, will naturally have moments of losing focus on the coachee and being at Level I. The practice for coaches is to return to connection with coachees at Levels II and III as quickly as possible.

Level I Dialogue

Coachee: The new house is a mess. I've got boxes everywhere. I can hardly get from the front door to the bathroom—and I've got the biggest proposal of my career to finish by Friday.

COACH: I went through the same thing last year. The key is to make sure you've got your long-term vision in sight.

Coachee: Uh. Okay, and that's sort of the dilemma, though. Because I traveled so much last month, my wife's past the point of patience. I'm really not pulling my weight at home.

COACH: Trust me. That'll work out. The mess is temporary. Don't let it distract you from the real issue: maintaining momentum.

Coachee: This feels like more than a little distraction.

COACH: I'm sure you can explain why this is so important. In the meantime, let's get back to your proposal.

Coachee: Okay. If you're sure . . .

Clearly, the coach is listening at Level I—paying more attention to his or her own judgments and opinions and driving for the coach's own conclusion. The point of this example is not which course of action is correct for this coachee but where the coach is focusing attention. In this case, the coach's attention is on a problem and the coach's predetermined solution to the problem, rather than on a coachee with a dilemma.

For leaders and managers, there's another version of listening at Level 1 that sometimes takes place internally. While the leader appears to be listening and may even be smiling in an encouraging way, the inner dialogue is *How much longer do I have to stand here before I can politely leave? I can't believe this is still an issue. We should have hired outside. I've got a phone call in 15 minutes I need to prepare for.* And so on.

Don't kid yourself. The person you are talking to can feel the difference between genuine listening and faux listening, and it has a negative impact. We've all been trained to decode these clues since we were children. No doubt you've been on the receiving end of that kind of disconnected listening yourself. A conversation where the person you're talking to is listening at Level 1 feels disengaged and inauthentic, and it ultimately undermines trust.

Level II: Focused Listening

At Level II, there is a sharp focus on the other person. Sometimes you can see it in each person's posture: both people are leaning forward and looking intently at each other. There is a great deal of attention on the other person and not much awareness of the outside world.

Let's go back to the restaurant scene and the two lovers. Dinner has been ordered, the menus taken away. Now their eyes are focused on each other and nothing else. They are so oblivious to the outside world that this scene of complete romantic isolation has become a caricature used in commercials. It's as if they're living in their own bubble.

When you, as a coach, are listening at Level II, your awareness is totally on your coachees. You listen for their words, their expressions, their emotions, everything they bring. You notice what they say, how they say it. You notice what they don't say. You see their smiles or hear the tears in their voices. You listen for what they value. You listen for their vision, for the unique way they look at the world. You listen for what makes them come alive in the coaching session and what makes them go dead or withdraw.

Energy and information come from the coachee. These are processed by the coach and reflected back. At Level II, the impact of awareness is on the coachee. The coach is like a perfect mirror that absorbs none of the light; what comes from the coachee is returned. At Level II, coaches are constantly aware of the impact their listening is having on their coachees. They are not constantly monitoring the impact, but they are aware. For the coach, everything you need to know about where to go next in the coaching just happened—a second ago—if you are listening and aware.

Level II listening is the level of empathy, clarification, collaboration. It is as if there is a wired connection between coach and coachee. At this level, coaches are unattached to self, their agenda, their thoughts, or their opinions. At Level II, coaches are so focused on the coachee that the mind chatter virtually disappears and coaching becomes spontaneous. As a coach, you are no longer trying to figure out the next move. In fact, if your attention is on trying to come up with what to say next—what brilliant question to pose to the coachee—that should be a clue that you are listening at Level l, inside your own experience.

As a coach listening at Level II, you not only hear the coachee speak but also notice all that is coming to you in the form of information—the tone, the pace, the feelings expressed. You choose what to respond to and how you will respond. Then you notice the impact of your response on the coachee and receive that information as well. It's as though you listen twice before the coachee responds again. You listen for the coachee's initial conversation, and you listen for the coachee's reaction to your response. You receive information both times. This is listening at Level II.

Leaders and managers should note that the ability to listen at this level is not limited to a private, confidential coaching session behind closed doors. It can apply to any conversation you have with colleagues or direct reports. Listening in this way requires consciousness and may need practice, but the key is awareness. It's as if time slows down and the surrounding noise is dimmed while you intently turn your attention to that person. When you connect at Level II, it's as if the message is *I have time for you.* Not just *I have time to address the problem* but *I have time for* you.

In describing Level II listening, we tend to use illustrations of one coach and one coachee, but Level II listening is about the focus of the awareness. For coaches who work with business partners, couples, or even teams, it is entirely possible to listen at Level II to more than one individual.

Level II Dialogue

Coachee: The new house is a mess. I've got boxes everywhere. I can hardly get from the front door to the bathroom—and I've got the biggest proposal of my career to finish by Friday.

COACH: What's that like?

Coachee: You mean, living in a pile of boxes?

COACH: I was thinking more about the dilemma that puts you in— pulled to honor an important career opportunity on the one hand and a family commitment on the other.

Coachee: Exactly. It feels like I'm going to let somebody down. Like I have to choose who to disappoint. I know if I don't help out with moving, I could be living solo soon, if you know what I mean. My wife did nearly all the packing last month while I was traveling.

COACH: It sounds like you've got this set up as *either/or*. There are only two choices, and no matter which way you play it, you lose.

Coachee: That's what it feels like.

COACH: I want to acknowledge your care in the process of making an important decision. At the moment it sounds like you're stuck between two options.

Coachee: I feel trapped—like there is no way out.

COACH: Let's take a step back. What's a third option? Thinking outside the box?

Here the coach is listening at Level II—following a deeper thread that is about how the coachee approaches the issue. The coach senses there is a more resourceful process possible that not only will address the current dilemma but could also lead to awareness that can be applied to other dilemmas in the future. For leaders and managers, even brief interactions like this can be an opportunity to support personal development for the employee or team member. When people feel listened to in this way, it communicates a deeper sense of support, commitment, and encouragement. If one of your goals as a leader is improved employee engagement, one option might be a focus on modeling Level II listening.

Level III: Global Listening

When you listen at Level III, you listen as if you and the coachee are at the center of the universe, receiving information from everywhere at once. It's as though you are surrounded by a force field that contains you, the coachee, and an environment of information. Level III includes everything you can observe with your senses: what you see, hear, smell, and feel—the tactile as well as the emotional sensations. Level III includes the action, the inaction, and the interaction.

If Level II is hardwired or laser focused, then Level III is like a radio field. The radio waves are entirely invisible, yet we trust they exist because we hear music coming from the radio. In Level III listening, we are hearing the radio waves. They cross our antennae and become information we can use. But it takes a special receiver to pick up Level III, and most people need practice because they don't often make use of Level III awareness the way a coach does. This may be a new realm of listening.

One of the benefits of learning to listen at Level III is greater access to your intuition. Through your intuition, you receive information that is not directly observable, and you use that information just as you would use words coming from the coachee's mouth. At Level III, intuition is simply more information. As a coach, you take in the information and respond. Then you notice the impact. How did your response land? What did you notice about that?

Level III awareness is sometimes described as environmental listening. You notice the temperature, the energy level, the lightness or darkness, both literally and figuratively. Is the coachee's energy sparking or flat? Is she cool, distant, . . . or on fire? Like a butterfly ready to fly off? Or a hawk with its talons gripping tightly? You will know by listening at Level III. You'll learn to trust your senses about that, and you can always just ask: "I get the sense that you're in an awkward place. Are you? What's that about?"

Performers develop a strong sense of Level III listening. Stand-up comedians, musicians, actors, training presenters—all have the ability to instantly read a room and monitor how it changes in response to what they do. This is a great example of noticing one's impact. Anyone who is successful at influencing people is skilled at listening at Level III. These people have the ability to read their impact and adjust their behavior accordingly.

Think about the impressive, inspiring leaders you've known or observed. It's almost certain they were skilled at Level III listening—awareness and impact and the ability to dance with whatever just happened. Reading the environment is a key leadership competence.

To listen at Level III, you must be very open and softly focused, sensitive to subtle stimuli, ready to receive information from all the senses—in your own sphere, in the world around you, in the world around your coachee. In some cases, that coachee is not just one person; it's the whole team. The environment itself is giving you information you can use in your coaching even when you can't instantly articulate what it is you are sensing. Sometimes this environment is shouting; sometimes it is whispering.

Level III Dialogue

Coachee: The new house is a mess. I've got boxes everywhere. I can hardly get from the front door to the bathroom—and I've got the biggest proposal of my career to finish by Friday.

COACH: I think I just heard alarms going off.

Coachee: Really?

COACH: Well, not literally. But you're talking very fast and it sounds like you're out of breath. That's not your usual tone. I get the sense that you're packed as tight as some of those boxes.

Coachee: Is it that obvious?

COACH: Like the walls are closing in. Cue the dramatic music.

Coachee: That's what it feels like—and with no way out. Cornered. In my relationship and in my work.

COACH: What do you want to do about that?

Coachee: What I've been trying to do is step around it, or over it, and that doesn't seem to be working. I guess it's time to sit down and work it out—unpack it all, so to speak.

In this case, the coach is tuned in at Level III: the nuances of the space between coach and coachee, beyond the words, including all the energy and emotion that were spoken and unspoken. Note that in the dialogue samples, we crafted the conversation to illustrate the distinctions between the three levels. In actual coaching conversations, of course, coaches switch constantly between Levels II and III—and when they slip into that Level I place, they recover as quickly as possible.

This mobility between Levels II and III is just as true for the conversations that leaders and mangers have when the opportunity for a coach-like conversation occurs. Naturally, we are not suggesting you make a conscious choice in the middle of the conversation: *I think I'll switch to Level III listening here.* That internal decision-making process would actually take you away from your connection with the employee. You'd be listening at Level I. No matter what caused the disconnect that created your Level I moment, the goal is to recover by reconnecting at Level II and Level III.

The Coach Is Listening

Everything in coaching hinges on listening—especially listening with the coachee's plan and purpose in mind: Is the coachee on track with his vision or learning objectives? Is she living her values? Where is he today? The coach is listening for signs of life, the choices coachees are making, and how those choices move them toward their desired future or away from it. The coach is also listening for resistance and turbulence in the process.

Listening is the entry point for the coaching. In one sense, all the other contexts depend on listening at Levels II and III. Listening, then, is the gateway through which all the coaching passes.

For leaders, there is a particular aspect to listening that focuses on the employee's development path. In a traditional coaching relationship between a trained coach and coachee, the outcome is centered on the goals of the coachee. In the case of leaders and managers there is a dual outcome: you help the coachee achieve important results, and, at the same time, you develop your own leadership skills and abilities that ultimately serve both the employee and the organization.

The key here is to make the distinction between addressing the issue at hand and coaching the person. It requires the ability to listen in a way that hears both options as potential directions to pursue. It is an essential part of a leader's listening process. Ask yourself, *What part of the issue just needs to be handled efficiently with my resource or answer?* and *Where in this conversation is there a development and learning opportunity?*

Any conversation can reveal a learning opportunity; in that moment there is a coach/leadership role available. This is where a coaching mind-set is transformative. When leaders and managers shift from managing the problem to managing the person, the cultural impact is enormous. It creates a clear, organizational value for employee growth and contribution. Employees are more engaged; they also take more initiative and responsibility. It's a triple win for the employee, manager, and organization.

Here is a simple example that illustrates how each of the two focus options might unfold:

Handling the Issue

> **Employee:** We have three potential suppliers to choose from. Two we have worked with in the past. All three are qualified. We've used Montgomery mostly.
>
> **MANAGER:** Are prices comparable? Can they deliver on time?
>
> **Employee:** Montgomery is a little more expensive, but their track record for delivery is better.

MANAGER: That's a plus. What feedback have you gotten from manufacturing?

Managing/Coaching the Person

Employee: We have three potential suppliers to choose from. Two we have worked with in the past. All three are qualified. We've used Montgomery mostly.

MANAGER: What part of this decision do you want help with?

Employee: To be honest, I'm uneasy about selecting Montgomery again.

MANAGER: What's the uneasiness about?

Employee: We had a problem with a recent order. It hasn't really been addressed. I still think we were overcharged.

MANAGER: Sounds like it could be a difficult conversation to have. What's the stretch in this for you?

Even in this brief dialogue example, it is clear there are two different pathways the manager can follow. One pathway leads rather directly to factors relevant for sorting out the choice of a supplier. The other pathway focuses on the opportunity to support this employee's development into a more confident and capable decision maker. In this second pathway, the current issue is resolved, and the employee is more empowered and resourceful in future situations. For the manager it all starts by listening with an ear to hear both potential pathways.

As coaches and leaders listen, they make choices that change the direction and focus of coaching. That's what we mean by the *impact* of listening. This impact shows up in the spontaneous choice of which coaching skill to use next.

Coaching Skills

The following coaching skills are generally associated with the context of listening. Of course, effective listening is a prerequisite for the use of all the coaching skills. For this section, we selected the skills that seem to be particularly appropriate responses to a listening situation.

Articulating

This skill is also known by a longer name: "Articulating what's going on." With your listening skills at Level II and Level III fully engaged, you have a heightened sense of awareness. You have a picture of what is going on with the coachee at this moment. When you combine that sense of what is happening right now with what you know about this coachee, you have a tremendous amount of information. Articulation is the ability to succinctly describe what is going on. Coachees often can't see for themselves what they are doing or saying. Or perhaps they can see the details but not the bigger picture.

With this skill, you share your observations as clearly as possible, but without judgment. You tell coachees what you see them doing. Sometimes, articulation takes the form of the hard truth, and it can confront: "I see you're continuing to schedule evening and weekend time away from your family. You've said in the past that your family is a high priority, and this overtime work seems inconsistent with that commitment. What's up?" By not sidestepping the apparent disconnect between personal promise and actual behavior, you live up to your coaching commitment. Articulating—as in pointing out the disconnect—is part of the coach's job. Cleaning up the mess is the coachee's job.

Articulating is a skill that helps coachees connect the dots so they can see the picture they are creating by their action or, sometimes, lack of action. As the coach, you have a responsibility to articulate what you see but at the same time, as with all of the coaching skills, not feel attached to being right about it. This ability to boldly say what you see without needing to be right, allowing plenty of room for counteroffers and different interpretations, is key to the co-active nature of the skill. As long as coaches can let go of the pressure or the need to be right, there is tremendous freedom to speak what appears to be true—and it is a great gift to coachees to hear this expressed.

Sample Dialogue

Coachee/Employee: . . . So I made some adjustments to my plan. I think it's a reasonable alternative. I think I can make the deadlines they've set for Phase 2 review.

COACH/MANAGER: Can I tell you what it sounds like from over here?

Coachee/Employee: Sure. You see a hole in there somewhere?

COACH/MANAGER: Actually, no. I'm sure the plan is sound. You're very thorough. What I see, though, is an old pattern of accommodating other people's demands, almost no matter how unreasonable those demands actually are, at personal cost to you. I also see that this is sometimes disruptive for the rest of our team. It's one of the things you said you wanted to change. This looks like backpedaling.

Clarifying

Many of us have a tendency to operate from vague or incomplete thoughts and unresolved feelings. We may leap to conclusions or draw conclusions based on sketchy information. Coachees may ramble or get caught up in their own stories. They may be drifting in a fog, trying to paddle their way out. They get stuck in fuzzy thinking and outdated ways of looking at their world. They may be reading old maps. Coaches serve as a resource to help coachees create greater clarity.

The skill of clarifying is a combination of listening, asking, and reframing. Sometimes it's simply testing different perspectives: "Here's what I'm hearing . . . " "Is that right?" "It sounds like you're looking for . . . " Clarifying brings the image into sharper focus, adds detail, and holds it up for inspection so the coachee can say, "Yes! That's it!" It's a way to move past the fog and get back on course.

Sample Dialogue

Coachee: . . . Unless he decides to go to New York. In that case, I'll stay here, at least for a while.

COACH: It sounds like there are two separate decisions for you to make, maybe three, and they're more dependent on what he does than on what you want. Help me out here.

Coachee: It sounds like I'm waiting for him to make his move before I make my decision.

COACH: And it sounds like you need to decide (a) whether you want that job at all, and (b) whether it's worth uprooting your life to have it, and then maybe (c) whether the relationship is sustainable. Or something like that.

Coachee: Sustainable under what conditions, really. Okay. I've got some work to do here.

Meta-View

Get in the imaginary helicopter with the coachee, take it up to about 10,000 feet, and look down on the coachee's life. This is the coaching skill of meta-view. It is especially useful when the coachee is in a rut and can only see six feet of dirt on each side. Meta-view presents the big picture and opens up room for perspective. The coach might ask: "What do you see from up here? What's the truth you can see from this vantage point that you couldn't see down there?" The meta-view reconnects coachees to their vision of themselves and a fulfilling life. When they're struggling at the foot of the mountain, looking up at the daunting work to be done, meta-view allows them to float above it and get a fresh perspective.

Another way to look at the meta-view is to see it as an elevated platform—a high place where coaches can stand to survey the coachee's life with all its circumstances and issues. The coach can see more than the coachee can from this vantage point. In fact, that is the coach's job: to maintain clarity of perspective and hold the big picture. This platform allows the coach to speak from outside the details of the immediate conversation.

A manager might recognize a pattern in how direct reports handle certain situations—a pattern they have recognized and talked about in the past. Taking on the coaching role for the moment, the manager might observe, "I can see where this topic is going and I'm happy to help, but let's push the pause button for a moment. In the big picture of this project—and with your desire to take more initiative and more leadership—what's your biggest challenge?

Another example might be the coachee who appears to be making a great effort but never gets anywhere. There is often a great deal of thrashing motion but not so much forward motion. In this case, the coach might invoke a meta-view this way: "There seems to be a lot of struggle. It seems to be a pattern. What are you getting out of all this struggle? What's the payoff?" In this last example, the meta-view is from a higher level that captures the underlying theme. Meta-view presents a panoramic view of the journey.

Meta-view is a useful way to provide context, especially when the situation makes it easy to be drawn into the details of a problem. For example, a coachee comes to the coaching session worried about the reaction she expects over the upcoming firing of a team member. The coach asks her to look at the situation from the meta-view—from the point of view of building a work culture—rather than focusing on hurt feelings or upsets. What are the costs to the organization of not firing that person? How will the firing affect communication and trust among coworkers in the long run?

Metaphor

The skill of metaphor enables you to draw on imagery and experience to help the coachee comprehend more quickly and more easily. The question "Are you drifting in a fog?" creates a picture, an experience that engages the coachee at a very different level than "Are you confused?" which addresses the coachee's intellect. Coachees can step into a picture of drifting in a fog. They know what it looks like and feels like. It's a whole experience. Metaphor provides rich imagery for exploration, and if the metaphor doesn't hit the mark in a way that increases insight, coaches can always try something else.

Acknowledging

The coaching skill of acknowledgment strengthens the coachee's foundation. The coachee can stand straighter after a true acknowledgment. This skill addresses who the coachee is. By way of contrast, praise and compliments highlight what people *do*: "Good job on that report, Janet." Or they highlight the opinion of the person giving the praise or the impact on the person giving the compliment: "Your presentation was thoughtful and inspiring to me."

Acknowledgment recognizes the inner character of the person to whom it is addressed. More than what that person did, or what it means to the sender, acknowledgment highlights who the sender sees: "Janet, you really showed your commitment to learning." "You took a big risk." "I can see your love of beauty in it." Acknowledgment often highlights a value that coachees honored in taking the action. The coachee values fun: "You made it really fun for yourself." Or the coachee values honesty: "I see a person who consistently takes a stand for honesty and authenticity—and it wasn't easy."

Acknowledgment is almost a context of coaching. At some level, coaches are always supporting who coachees must be in order to make the changes they say they want to make. The coachee had to be courageous, or had to be a person willing to stand up to the fear, or had to be tenacious for the sake of a relationship.

The skill of acknowledgment helps the coach celebrate the coachee's internal strengths. Acknowledgment helps coachees see what they sometimes dismiss in themselves out of a distorted sense of humility, or simply don't see at all. By acknowledging that strength, you, as the coach, give coachees more access to it. Coachees will know when the acknowledgment is honest and true. They will be more resourceful in the future because they recognize the truth you illuminated.

Acknowledgment might take this form: "It sounds like you surprised yourself. But think about how far you've come in the past four months. Your ability to be clear and take a stand demonstrates the presence of leadership you said you wanted to see in yourself." Acknowledgment goes right to the heart of where the coachee is growing and getting stronger (and, often, feeling the need for validation). When you acknowledge this, you empower coachees to keep growing.

There are actually two parts to every acknowledgment in co-active coaching. The first part we've already covered: delivering the acknowledgment. The second part is noticing the impact on the coachee. This is a way for the coach to make sure that the acknowledgment was truly on target. Notice the coachee's reaction. By listening at Level III, you will know if you found the right description of who the coachee had to be in that situation. The acknowledgment will definitely land in a way you can hear, sense, and see. It is enormously moving—and rare—for coachees to be seen and known in this way. That's the power of acknowledgment.

Sample Dialogue

Coachee: Maybe I should have kept my mouth shut. It just gets me into trouble.

COACH: You stir things up. That's what you do. That's who you are. You are not the complacent one, the one hiding undercover hoping the storm will pass. As you have said in the past, sometimes that means you're the lightning rod.

Coachee: Thanks. I may never get the "Most Popular Team Member" award, but I can see that my willingness to be a lightning rod can make a real contribution.

Exercises

1. Listening at Level I

The goal of this exercise is to listen completely at Level I: to remain focused entirely on your own thoughts and opinions. To do this exercise, ask a friend or colleague to play the Level I and Level II listening games with you.

Describe Level I listening to your partner. Then ask that person to describe a trip he or she took, including stories about things that went well and things that didn't go so well. As your partner tells the story of the trip, your job is to listen to the words and interpret the story entirely in terms of your own experience. Make frequent comments in which you offer your opinion. Describe how you would have done the trip differently. Be sure to include stories from trips you have taken. Ask yourself, *What does my friend's story remind me of in my own life?*

After five or 10 minutes (if you last that long), tell each other what it was like to listen at Level I and what it was like to be listened to at Level I.

2. Listening at Level II

Work with the same partner—and the same story—for another five to 10 minutes. But this time, without describing Level II, be curious. Ask questions, clarify, and articulate what you see. Be alert for your partner's values as they are expressed in the story. Stay completely focused on your partner by listening and responding at Level II.

Tell each other what it was like to listen at Level II and what it was like to be listened to at Level II. How was the experience different from the Level I listening?

3. Listening at Level III

Take a field trip or two to venues where the Level III activity is likely to be noticeable, such as a library, a hotel lobby, a restaurant. Pay attention to your awareness at Level III. Notice how people are feeling: angry, frustrated, joyful, bored, at peace, anxious? What else do you notice about the environment? What is the buzz in the room? Notice where the energy is in the room and how it shifts as people arrive or depart. Write down your impressions. Then try listening at Level III with your eyes closed. How is it different? What do you note that you didn't notice with your eyes open? Compare a church sanctuary to a fast-food restaurant. What are the differences as you listen at Level III?

Variation: Have a friend enter the room clearly annoyed and angry. Notice how the room reacts at Level III. Or have two friends enter the room and start a loud, rude conversation. Notice how the Level III energy changes.

4. Meta-View

A meta-view is the big picture. It is part theme, part positioning statement, and part vision. An easy way to practice meta-view is to start a sentence with "I am ..." or "My life is ..."

Here are some examples of metaviews:

I am ...

- Launching a new life
- Stuck in transition
- Escaping the prison
- Struggling with change
- Creating a new organizational culture

My life is ...

- A high-speed action machine (some parts are falling off)
- Peacefully unfolding
- Filled with questions without answers

What is the meta-view for your own life today? Write down the names of 10 close friends or relatives. What is the meta-view for each of them at this time?

5. Metaphor

Create a metaphor for each of the following coachee situations:

- Stuck between two appealing choices
- About to enter an exciting new period with a lot of unknowns
- After a long period of inaction, everything happening at once
- Chaotic work environment
- Two new romantic relationships
- Money losses because of mismanagement
- Going from too little exercise to overdoing it
- Making great progress building the business until the interruption
- Success
- Sadness
- Series of windfalls
- Exhaustion
- Denial

6. Acknowledging

List five friends or coworkers. Write an acknowledgment of who they are or who they have been in order to get to where they are today. Write an acknowledgment for yourself.

CHAPTER 4

Intuition

Maybe you've had an experience like this: You're driving in the country on back roads that aren't marked very well. You come to an intersection of two roads and instinctively turn to the right, trusting your sense of direction. Or this may have happened: You're having dinner with a friend. Everything seems normal on the surface. The conversation has its usual flow. Seemingly from nowhere you get an urge to ask, "Is there something you need to tell me?" For you, there was something you sensed—that you didn't have words for—that seemed out of tune. You might call it a gut feeling.

Gut feelings happen at work, too. Imagine this scenario: You have an important position to fill, and you have three excellent candidates. On paper, one candidate stands out for his credentials and experience, but it just doesn't feel right to you. Your instinct tells you the right choice is the third candidate you interviewed. You have a strong feeling you trust, but it also means you'll need to have a convincing rationale for your instinct. How will you justify a "gut feeling" to HR and your boss?

That's often the case with intuition; in the moment it feels more reliable than the data, the analysis, and all the usual tidy columns of pros and cons. It arrives as an impulse that is often ignored or discredited because it's not logical and therefore not viewed as credible.

And yet intuition can be enormously valuable as a powerful, additional channel for information, which is why we include it as one of the five contexts in the co-active approach to coaching conversations. When that channel is available and open, intuition has the potential to accelerate a process and deepen the conversation in ways that are sometimes surprising. To the toolkit of analysis, evaluation, and a structured process for addressing an issue, we simply add this additional dimension for what often amounts to a shortcut.

We have words to define intuition, but the actual experience is sometimes hard to explain—"Where did that come from?"—which makes it difficult for some to accept. For many people, the trouble with intuition starts with the difficulty of verifying that it's "real." Sometimes there's no observable evidence for the conclusion. In some cases, the conclusions people derive from their intuition are actually contrary to observable evidence. People who operate from their intuition will say things like "I know because my intuition is usually right about these things."

Those who have trouble believing in intuition frequently treat it as guessing or being lucky. They don't understand, trust, or believe in intuition. Facts that can be measured, recorded, verified—that's what people frequently say they want. It's the culturally approved method for making important decisions. People are comfortable with that process.

Intuition, on the other hand, might appear to be too weird or unprofessional, so people are sometimes shy about admitting they have used their intuition. Even those with intuition in abundance are often reluctant to admit they have used it, and so this ability atrophies. That's too bad, because it's a powerful asset in coaching—and in life generally for that matter.

Both a rational mind and an intuitive gut feeling access information. Neither approach is the right or wrong way; they provide information from different sources. A rational mind is weighted toward analysis and logic, which we all agree can be very useful in business and in life. Gut feelings are weighted toward creative possibility and innovation—thinking outside the box—a resource that is also very useful in business and in life. As human beings, we have been given the gift of both approaches. We can be thoughtful and we can be inspired. We are most effective when we have access to both approaches and have the creative capacity to navigate between them.

Another Word for *Intuition*

Within the walls of most organizations, using a phrase like "My intuition tells me . . . " might sound out of place and might not be thought of as business-like. In that case, maybe an alternative word would be *instinct*, as in, "My instinct tells me . . . " For the purposes of understanding this co-active context and its use, imagine that the two words basically refer to the same thing, and use the word you are most comfortable with.

As leader or manager, you may be accustomed to trusting your instinct in certain areas based in large part on your experience. It's a level of knowing that processes a great deal of data at once in cluster, not linearly.

Instinct might come into play in any co-active conversation. Imagine a conversation between a doctor and a nurse. They're reviewing a patient's condition, looking for a clear care path forward, checking the chart and vital signs—and at the same time being open to intuition based on experience. Their conversation can now include a professional instinct based on a feeling that "something is not quite right." Intuition in this case could play a critical role.

When the conversation is a coaching dialogue, there is an essential shift for the coach, manager, or leader from "what my instinct tells me about this situation" to "what is happening in the moment in our conversation." You may have a strong instinct about the best direction to take to solve the problem at hand. However, in a co-active context, the purpose for instinct is to support the coachee; it is not instinct for the purpose of giving advice.

When you find that your attention is on figuring out the solution, shift to the person and the conversation in front of you. In this case, instinct might sound like "It feels like we're circling the issue." Or "My instinct tells me there's a key piece missing. I just don't have words for it." Or "My sense is, we're using the wrong tool to fix this."

Instinct or intuition are not necessarily the first place we go for information or inspiration. We're trained to analyze, hypothesize, size things up, and propose action steps. However, it might be that a "stuck place" is the most useful place to be in, in order to practice your instinct or intuition. You have nothing to lose; the usual process isn't working, so look outside the box. Try something bold.

The Known versus the Unknown Universe

Most of us have come to believe that the known universe is within hand's reach. It is within our field of vision, our range of hearing, accessible to our five senses. A thing is known when others corroborate it and come up with the same data. Intuition, however, is not directly observable—although sometimes its effects are. Like the wind in the trees, it may not be visible, but we can see and hear its effects. That's why it is sometimes called the "sixth sense." It is a sensitivity that goes beyond the physical world.

Suppose someone says, "It's going to rain today." You ask, "How do you know?" The answer might include one or all of the following:

I heard the National Weather Service report on the radio.

There was a red sky this morning.

The barometer on the wall has been dropping fast all morning.

The wind is from the east and clouds are building in the west.

I feel it in my bones.

In fact, some people really do feel approaching rain in their bones. The point is that there are many ways of knowing. One of those ways is scientifically verifiable evidence, but there is also "just knowing." When you look at this list of possible answers, you might want to ask, *Which source is right?* A different question would be, *Which one do I trust?* Many people would say there's a direct relationship between what they can observe and their confidence in knowing. For these people, their trust is in the concrete experience. They would also say that intuition is way down on the trust scale—maybe even 0 percent for reliability.

But instead of insisting that there is only one form of knowing, let's suppose there are two. Conventional, observable knowing is one form; intuition is the second. Together these two dimensions give depth and perspective to any issue.

But Is It Right?

Part of the difficulty of describing intuition as a way of knowing starts with the definition of *knowing*. One way of looking at intuition says that it is neither right nor wrong—it's more like a nudge we receive. For example, answer these questions: *What day of the week is tomorrow? What is tomorrow's date? What season will it be tomorrow? What will the weather be like during this particular season in this particular year? What's your theme during this season of your life in this particular year?*

Notice that the answer to each question is found in a different place. One of the places is your memory; another place is your logical mind; another place is your history. And perhaps another place is your intuition. What if intuition were a place—not a place we visit often, perhaps, but simply a place that we go to, like memory, that provides us with an answer? We take the nudge and give it expression.

In order to express our intuition in words, we make an interpretation. It's our interpretation of the intuitive nudge that can be off-target. The intuitive impulse itself is neither right nor wrong. Imagine this scenario: Your coachee is in the midst of a report about the action she took last week. It's a great report, with one success after another. She's followed through on everything just as she said she would. But your intuition senses a "disturbance in the force" that you interpret as, "She's holding something back." So despite the overwhelming evidence of accomplishment, you say, "My intuition tells me there's something you're not saying about last week. Is that true?"

Your intuition gave you a nudge. Your interpretation is that the coachee is holding back, so that's what you say. It doesn't matter whether you are right or wrong about your interpretation. If the coachee is holding back, then great; you opened a door to talk about that. If the coachee says she isn't holding anything back, then great; you reinforce the success story. The thing about intuition and coaching is that intuition always forwards the action and deepens the learning, even when it lands with a *clang* instead of a melodious *ping*.

Intuition often shows up in unexpected ways in the coaching conversation. Sometimes it's a hunch. Or it might appear as a visual image or an unexplained shift in emotion or energy. The important thing to remember in coaching is to be open to intuition—trusting it, aware of it, and completely unattached to the interpretation. In the end, intuition is valuable when it moves the coachee to action or deeper learning. It is irrelevant, really, whether your intuition was "correct."

Sample Dialogues

Example A: Something Overlooked

Coachee: It's like I've run out of options, and I'm worn out. Doing the same things over and over, talking to the same people, showing the same old résumé. Even when the faces and names change, it's all a repeat performance.

COACH: My intuition tells me there's something else—something that's been overlooked. Like it's right there in front of you but you don't see it. What could that be?

Coachee: I don't know. I feel like I've been going down this road for so long that I'm in a rut.

COACH: The road's a good image; let's work with that. Imagine there's a fence running along this road, and there's a gate in the fence. What's the gate?

Coachee: It's the road not taken.

COACH: And where does that road lead? If you were going to make something up, what would that be?

Coachee: Actually, it reminds me of my grandparents' home in Connecticut. My grandfather is the only person in our family who worked for himself. I thought he was about the smartest man alive to be able to do that. I really admired his independence.

COACH: What does the gate mean to you in your own life?

Coachee: That gate's always been there—and I've always walked past, because I thought I wanted security. This could be the time for me to take a serious look at what it would be like to create my own sense of security, working for myself.

Example B: Drawing on Coachee Interest

Coachee/Employee: . . . By the end of the third quarter. Which means I will need to just about double my output—comparing last year to this year. I really want to hit the mark, I really do, but I just don't see how it's possible.

WORKPLACE COACH: How would the marathon runner do it?

Coachee/Employee: Where did that come from?

WORKPLACE COACH: Intuition, I guess. You once told me you ran a marathon. Isn't that right?

Coachee/Employee: I did. Years ago.

WORKPLACE COACH: So, looking at the task ahead as if it were a long-distance race, what do you know you need to do?

Coachee/Employee: That's easy. Draw up a schedule that builds steadily over time—like a long-distance training plan.

Intuitive Intelligence

Another way to think of intuition is to regard it as a kind of intelligence, like musical intelligence or visual intelligence. All of us who are not blind or color-blind can identify colors. We start in preschool, and many of us add to our color vocabulary over the years, becoming more adept at recognizing colors. Artists learn to identify and name many shades of colors. In their minds, they can picture the subtle differences between hundreds of shades. Intuition is like that. It is an intelligence everyone has been given in some measure, and we can develop it just as artists and musicians develop their talents.

The reference to artists and musicians is apt because they represent the creative process in real time. That's especially true with improvisation, where the music is being created one note at a time in the moment. The application to work in organizations is an awareness of the necessity for any team or team member in an organization to be open to a creative process. Intuition by its nature is inherently creative.

When the team is facing a particularly challenging issue, the ability to think outside the box—to improvise and generate new options and new possibilities–is key. The same thinking and problem-solving process that initially created the challenge the team now faces may not be enough to address the issue. The team may need to engage in radical reimagining and opening the channel to innovative, inspired, intuitive intelligence.

One of the interesting things about intuition is its elusive quality. Looking too intently for it makes it more difficult to find. If you are working too hard to find your intuition, then your attention is on you and your efforts. By shifting your attention to the question or the other person and opening the channel, you can more easily find the answer. The key seems to be to take a soft focus, to be open. Your intuition is there, giving you messages or clues, just below the surface. This is the paradox of intuition: an open hand will hold it; it will slip through a fist.

Observation and Interpretation

We have said that intuition starts with a nudge, a feeling. It could also be an observation, although it might not be clear that you have observed something specific. Calling it simply an *observation* makes it neutral. You can say "I have a feeling," or "I have an observation," or "I have an intuition," and no one can dispute it. It is your feeling, observation, or intuition. What happens next is often an interpretation of the feeling, intuition, or observation. We need to put some words around this very subjective nudge. It is natural to give the intuition a meaning, and it is this interpretation of the intuition that can be off-base.

For example, in listening to your coachee, you sense awkward hesitation. It could be avoidance; it could be resistance. Maybe that hesitation is related to the subject of this conversation. Then again, maybe it's completely unrelated—the coachee is distracted for some personal reason. Maybe it's about the way you asked the question or the fact that you're standing in the break room with this team member and not in a more private setting. There could be many explanations for the hesitation. Your intuition or your instinct tells you it's important to shine a light on it. Note that the nudge doesn't come with a descriptive label. It's a nudge—an impulse.

When you speak from that intuition you use words, and they are your best effort in the moment to package the nudge. You are communicating an observation—*and* you are also declaring an interpretation: in that hesitation it sounds like something is being held back. If you jump right to your interpretation, it will too often come out as a conclusion, an accusation, or a judgment. The coachee's job is to take the information you provide from your intuition and apply it to his or her situation. What fits? What doesn't fit? In the end, it is the coachee who comes up with the conclusion.

The lesson here is that if you're going to use your intuition effectively, you can't be attached to your interpretation. In fact, this desire to be right about an interpretation is often the reason people hold back their intuition. They're afraid of being wrong or appearing foolish.

The best approach is to be prepared. When you express your intuition, coachees may disagree. Even so, they will learn as much as if your intuition were somehow "correct." What was correct was the intuition to say something. What was correct was whatever the coachee learned. What's more, coachees count on your intuition. When you hold back, you withhold a crucial source of information and sensing. The key lesson: do not be attached to your intuition, no matter how certain you feel. Being attached to being right is something you do for your sake. Coaching is for the sake of the coachee.

Finding Your Own Access Point

We develop our ability to access our intuition in the same way we develop talents or build muscles. Intuitive fitness is just as possible as physical fitness. Fortunately, coaching is an intuition fitness gym. In practical terms, how do we find access to our intuition, especially if we're not accustomed to looking for it? It can be somewhat elusive. Compared to the triceps muscle, which is in the same place for all of us, our intuition is found in a different place for each of us.

Many people find their intuition in the body—in their chest or stomach. It's no wonder people talk of intuition as a "gut response" or a feeling "in my gut." Some feel a burning on the forehead or a tingling in the fingers. For others, intuition is not felt in the body at all. It may be above you, or it might be a bubble that surrounds you. You may "see" your intuition in a visual way or feel it kinesthetically. Some people find that they're better able to access their intuition by standing up. For others, the connection is definitely verbal. The next time you notice that your intuition or instinct is actively present, listen to your body or your experience at that point in time to locate where the communication is coming from.

Whatever your access point, eventually you'll need to verbalize the nudge from your intuition. You make sense out of the sensation by giving words to it. As coach, your responsibility is to speak what your intuition gives you. Your coachees get to decide what is useful about your intuitive nudge.

Intuition is a powerful asset in your coaching. It is well worth the practice to develop it, and the good news is that your intuition is always available, on standby. You don't have to generate it any more than you have to generate the electricity to run the lights in your office or home. You simply have to remember to turn it on.

Blurting It Out

Even after the nudge of intuition, there is often a natural tendency to hold back, to analyze it, to check and see if it is right or if this is the right time to say something or find the right words for it. Unfortunately, by the time you've performed a set of validation tests on your intuition, the conversation has moved on. Your moment is lost. Intuition is like a small flash of light that is already beginning to fade as soon as it appears. The most powerful moment is the first. Holding back out of fear and timidity, hesitating, will allow it to pass by. That's a shame, because blurting out your intuition can often create a dramatic shortcut in the coaching conversation, boring through many layers.

As coaches, we sometimes think we need to track the logical unfolding of a conversation, hooking together question and response and question and response in a neat sequence. This is an excellent way to build new learning and discovery with coachees, but it is not the only way. Being willing to risk a jump with your intuition, taking the chance you'll end up with either a beautiful dive or a horrendous splash, gives you another way to go directly to something you can feel in the conversation that you may not be able to fully articulate or logically diagram in the moment. This willingness to fail at it, bow in good humor, and press on gives you license to use your intuition with more freedom.

Getting the Intuitive Hit

Sometimes intuition comes in the form of words, but it could just as easily be in shapes or sounds, as a feeling or a body sensation. Your intuition might communicate to you through a sense of heaviness, an ache, or a mood. Sometimes the intuitive hint arises from the conversation itself.

Sometimes it is out there in the environment. A scene outside the office window might inspire an intuitive remark. The scene creates an image . . . which your intuition signals to you . . . and you share with your coachee . . . and then you see where it goes from there.

For example, imagine your coachee is describing her concerns about the impact of an upcoming reorganization in her area of responsibility. She wants to sort out the important issues, and she's wondering what the right course of action is. You look out the window and notice it is a crisp fall day, one of the first. It's a strong impression, and you mention it: "I'm noticing it's a beautiful fall day. The leaves are changing color; the air is cooler today. What does that bring up for you?" It might suggest a sense of the changing seasons in her life and give her the means for sorting out the changes before her. Or it could remind her of chores that need to be done to get ready for winter—action steps in preparation for big changes. The source of the intuition is irrelevant. What is relevant is what happens for the coachee.

Phrasing It

Here are some tips for expressing your intuition. You can use any of the following phrases to begin to express that intuitive nudge and, of course, this is not a definitive list. In fact, it's good practice to simply begin with one of these phrases, having no idea of what will come out of your mouth, trusting that your intuition will fill in the blanks as you go along.

> *I have a sense . . .*
> *May I tell you about a gut feeling I have?*
> *I have a hunch that . . .*
> *Can I check something out with you?*
> *I wonder if . . .*
> *See how this fits for you.*

And perhaps the best one of all is also the simplest and most direct:

> *My intuition tells me . . .*

Intuition is not magic, although sometimes it might feel like that, especially when we're delighted with the results. Intuition is like listening. It is a powerful talent that can help coachees move into action or deepen their learning.

Coaching Skills

The following coaching skills are associated with intuition, although they are not exclusive to that context. We chose these skills for this section because they naturally come from a place of intuition or help give intuition an opening for expression. We listed metaphor under the listening context, but it could just as easily be included here, since metaphor is often drawn from intuition.

Intruding

Because most coaching sessions are brief, it may be necessary to intrude on the coachee's report or storytelling in order to get to the heart of the matter. As coach, you use your Level III awareness to decide when it's time to do that. Rather than wait for a socially polite break in the conversation, you interrupt and redirect the conversation or ask a question. Often your intuition urges you to intrude. Note that it isn't necessary to be rude, although your interruption may be perceived by some as rude, especially in parts of the world where such behavior might be seen as disrespectful.

Remember, too, that coachees usually know when they're droning on and on. If you don't redirect this type of rambling, coachees begin to think of the coaching session as a place to tell stories, not get into action; before long they're dissatisfied and ready to abandon the coaching relationship. Coachees do not want to use up all their time in a coaching session with "and then I . . . " or "and she said . . . " Some coachees will also keep talking until you say something. In their desire to be good coachees or to be thorough, they keep pressing on, hoping you will intervene to get the conversation back on track.

In general, it's best if you prepare your coachees for these types of intrusions at the beginning of your coaching relationship. Explain that you'll sometimes interrupt the conversation in a way that may surprise them. Let them know that a coaching conversation is different from chit-chatting with a friend over coffee. You may need to interrupt, and you ask that they not take it personally. Ask them to let you know if they feel offended so that the two of you can talk about it again if necessary. This should be all the permission you need, as a coach, to intrude whenever it seems appropriate.

Maybe you still feel reluctant to intrude, thinking that it's not your style. Here's the real point: you're not intruding on them; you're intruding on the story that gets in the way—that obscures and fogs the picture. Would you really rather be perceived as polite, or nice, than intrude to help your coachees get to the heart of the matter? Remember that coaching is about the coachee, not the coach. Coaching is therefore not for the faint of heart.

Your job as coach is to work with whatever comes up and to leave your agenda and ego out of the conversation. However, there are times when you will need to take charge. Your experience and training in coaching give you the authority you need to serve the coachee. Holding back, being nice at this point, does not serve the coachee's best interests. There will be times when you'll have to jump in to clarify, make a strong request or pose a powerful challenge, or tell the hard truth. Since there is no hard-and-fast rule, this is a good place for trusting your intuition on when to intrude.

Coaches also sometimes fail to intrude because they believe they need more information, more background or context, before they can intervene with the next question. It's true that it is sometimes important to hear the story for its context. It may also be necessary so that coachees feel heard, listened to; in this case, it is important for the sake of the relationship. But we assume you are already skilled at listening well to the story. What many coaches need is more practice intruding. The skill of intruding helps cut off unnecessary reporting—which can be a defensive smoke screen put up by the coachee to avoid getting to the more challenging issues. Intruding accelerates the process of getting to the core: the action and the learning.

Sample Dialogues

Example A: Poor Use of the Skill of Intruding

Coachee/Employee: It's Mary again. She is so unbelievably contrary. If I say I think we should go east, she says no, we should head west.

If I say the only way to meet the deadline is to hire outside help, she says no, it's up to us, it just means we need better teamwork. Teamwork! What could be more hypocritical? Over and over I've asked her to be a more involved member of the team. She's off on her own track, not communicating, and then "surprise!" It's really irritating, and it's undermining the team.

COACH/MANAGER: It must be very frustrating. I know you've mentioned it before.

Coachee/Employee: *Really* frustrating. Did I tell you her latest? It gets better.

COACH/MANAGER: More of the same, I'm sure.

Coachee/Employee: Of course. It doesn't end . . . blah, blah, blah, blah, blah, blah, blah, blah.

Example B: Good Use of the Skill of Intruding

Coachee/Employee: It's Mary again. She is so unbelievably contrary. If I say I think we should go east, she says no, we should head west. If I say the only way to meet the deadline is to hire outside help, she says no, it's up to us . . .

COACH/MANAGER: Sounds like an endless battle of wills.

Coachee/Employee: I'll say.

COACH/MANAGER: What will change the game?

Coachee/Employee: Excuse me? I'm not sure what you mean.

COACH/MANAGER: What will it take to break the cycle?

Coachee/Employee: I don't know. I've tried talking with her.

COACH/MANAGER (Intuition): Let's start with this: what do you both care about?

Blurting

We've touched on the importance of blurting. Odd as it may sound, blurting is actually a skill worth developing. Most of us spend so much time trying to analyze and figure things out that in the delay, we miss the opportunity to jump in.

In coaching, it actually serves the coachee to go right into the messiness without sorting it out first. It's better to dive in and be willing to look a little clumsy. This often builds more trust than if you are always the polished, professional authority, always in control. Being clumsy or messy, and therefore more human, is also more authentic. And if you don't have to look good, your coachee doesn't have to look good either. For example, as coach you might say, "I'm not sure what the right words are here, but it's something like . . ." or "Let me just talk out loud for a minute. I'm not sure exactly what I want to say here."

Coachees and Their Intuition

It's worth noting that watching the coach work with intuition allows coachees to experiment and take risks with their own intuition. In fact, learning the coaching principles, contexts, and skills can be a great benefit to coachees. Coachees who become proficient at listening at Levels II and III, for example, have new skills to be much more effective in their relationships at work and at home. Learning to clarify, or to keep the meta-view, in their personal lives will be a tremendous advantage, too.

As you teach coachees to work with intuition, begin by asking them to spend time noticing their intuition and playing with it. You might ask them to simply experiment; this takes the pressure off trying to do it "right." Prepare them for the possible appearance of their internal skeptic—in addition to the external skeptics they are likely to encounter.

Exercises

1. Intuition

Intuition is the sixth sense that helps us respond to a question. Sometimes the question is explicit and posed; sometimes it's part of the background of the conversation. In coaching, there is always a question in the air.

To practice your intuition, meet with a friend or a colleague in a quiet place where the two of you can be undisturbed for a while. First, ask your partner to write down a series of open-ended questions about his or her life. Then have your partner choose one question from the list to read out loud a few times in a row, with a brief space of quiet between each repetition of the question. Next, take two or three minutes for both of you to concentrate on the question without speaking. Your goal is to increase your concentration on the question and open yourself to whatever your intuition offers.

At the end of the time period, tell your partner everything that occurred: the random thoughts; the feelings; anything you noticed in terms of visual images, sounds, smells, and touch; along with whatever else you may have noticed or anything that distracted you. Some of what you report from your intuition is sure to connect for the other person. As soon as that intuitive hit happens, ask what the connection is and explore that area for greater awareness.

You can double the intrigue in this exercise by having your partner write the questions on slips of paper and then fold the slips so the questions can't be read. Pick a piece of paper from the pile, keeping the question hidden. Then spend two or three minutes to each concentrate on the question you picked even though you haven't read it. Again, report whatever comes up from your intuition. Then read the question and ask your partner for comments. Where were the connections? Where does this lead?

2. Intruding

Sit down with a friend and let that person know that in order to practice the skill of intruding, you are going to interrupt as he or she talks. Have your friend tell a story from a significant period of his or her life. It could be a learning experience from school. It could be a story about meeting his or her best friend. Ask your friend to pick a story that can be stretched, since it's important that the story go on and on. As your friend is telling you the story, your job is to interrupt and change the course of the storytelling by using these coaching skills:

- Ask your friend to summarize: "What did that mean to you?"

- Interrupt with a provocative question (not a question for more information), such as "What did you learn from that?"
- Interrupt by articulating what is going on in the story at that moment.
- Interrupt with a request.
- Intrude by announcing your intention to interrupt: "I'm going to interrupt here."

Language for interrupting might include "Excuse me, you just …" or "Let me ask …"

CHAPTER 5

Curiosity

As a context for coaching, curiosity may be the quality that starts the process and the energy that keeps it going. The most effective coaches seem to be naturally curious and to have developed their curiosity in a way that opens doors and windows for coachees. Being genuinely curious and eager to play with whatever shows up is at the heart of a co-active relationship.

A Different Way of Asking

Curiosity starts with a question. The interesting thing about a question is that it automatically causes us to start looking. For example, when you read this question, "Is it cold outside today or hot?" chances are that you instantly started thinking about your local weather. We have this natural, automatic response to a question. It sends us looking for an answer. Simply posing the question shifts the trajectory of the conversation. One of the reasons coaching is a powerful agent for change is because of the emphasis on curiosity and the questions curiosity evokes.

Curious questions are open, expansive, provocative, and exploratory, sometimes piercing through many layers. They invite exploration, reflection, and discovery. They prompt a search for information but in a way that runs deeper than the usual, conventional information-gathering questions.

Our experience in school trained us to gather information by asking specific questions that enabled us to deduce answers. In that environment, we learned that questions have specific answers—in fact, right answers.

Even essay questions have correct answers that are specific, concrete, and measurable. We learned that questions are used to narrow the possibilities. This is the deductive method. We learned to fill in the blanks, and we learned about being scored on our ability to get the right answers.

That mind-set and habit carried over to life at work, too. In meetings and one-on-one interactions, questions mostly have a function to produce information or data. Anything more expansive is generally rare, which means that asking a curious question in a coaching conversation is an important—sometimes uneasy—shift.

Coachees are accustomed to answering questions from a surface place, a database of knowing that's easy to access. It's what they are prepared for; it's what they expect to be asked about and what they are ready to respond to. From their perspective, an open invitation to give an opinion or explore more deeply can feel personally vulnerable. It might even create a momentary pressure to try to come up with the "right" answer—especially if the question is coming from the boss.

And yet it is that very shift from the exchange of surface-level information to a deeper and more reflective discovery that makes the coaching interaction a powerful experience. There is a big difference between conventional questions that elicit information and curious questions that evoke personal exploration. The following examples illustrate the differences between the two types of questions.

Information Gathering	*Curious*
What products and geographies will you include in your market analysis?	What insight are you looking for from the market analysis?
How much exercise do you need each week?	What would "being fit" look like for you?
What cities are on your list as you consider your next move?	What's important to you about places where you might live?

The deadliest questions of all in this style of information gathering are the questions that ask for a yes or a no. They simply erect a huge stop sign in the middle of the conversation. The road ends abruptly, and the coach has to start all over again. Curious questions, however, are open-ended.

They take the coachee on a journey and are easily phrased to avoid sudden stops. Notice the differences in responses that could be elicited by the following types of questions:

Closed	*Open*
Is this an effective strategy for you?	What makes this an effective strategy for you?
Is there more to be learned here?	How can you double the learning in this experience?
It sounds like you're stuck between those two choices—is that true?	What's another option besides the two in front of you?

Notice in these examples the difference in the way the two different styles of questions make you feel. Close-ended, yes-or-no, information-gathering questions feel more restrictive. Curious questions feel more expansive.

Another form of the closed-ended question is the leading question. The leading question implies that there is a right answer, a conclusion, built into the question itself. But the leading question leaves little choice. It pretty much forces the learner to come up with the answer the teacher is looking for. The person asking is not actually curious; that question is masquerading as an opinion hidden in a question. Here are some examples.

- Have you thought about subdividing the sales territories to make them more fair?
- When you think about going back to school to get your PhD and accomplish your career dream, have you considered the emotional toll on your family and the debt burden it will create?

Just to be clear: There is definitely a valuable role for information-gathering questions. They are essential in everyday life and work situations. We couldn't survive long without them. The encouragement here is to notice the impact of the questions you ask—especially in a coaching conversation. *Where did that question send my coachee?*

Even in a coaching relationship, there are times when information gathering is important in order to stay on track or clarify when there is a potential for misunderstanding or confusion. Our point is this: the answers to information-gathering questions will give us the address on the door, but they don't open the door to a rich, rewarding experience of engaging conversation. Only curious questions will do that.

Culture Building

Curiosity as a co-active context has a special place in organizations. It is a leadership competency as well as a coaching skill. That observation comes from witnessing the impact that conversations have on the culture of the organization. The sort of conversations people have reveals—and simultaneously creates—the organizational culture. Think about your own experience. An organization that spends a lot of energy blaming creates a toxic culture where no one is accountable. When things don't go according to plan, it's always someone else's responsibility or somebody else's fault.

An organization or team that communicates strictly on a functional basis of information exchange creates a transactional culture. This is not a judgment as much as it is an inquiry: what sort of culture do you want to create? (That might be a leading question.) A co-active culture values—and by practice creates—a culture that is both in relationship and in action. It is transactional in the sense of getting things done, moving forward, and it is relational. It creates the container and support for mutual benefit.

The Value of Curiosity

In our co-active model, curiosity includes both the questions we ask and the curious mind-set we bring to the conversation. The curious coach doesn't have all the answers. In fact, you're clueless. When you are curious, you are no longer in the role of expert. Instead, you are joining coachees in a quest to find out what's there. You are exploring their world with them, not superimposing your world on theirs. It is like looking at their world through the wondering eyes of a child.

As a consultant, you gather information so that you can come up with appropriate recommendations. You have the expertise, and you are casting for information to determine where to go. You're like a general contractor who has been hired to come in and build an addition to the house with the materials you bring to the site. In co-active coaching, in contrast, you are curious. You come in as a collaborator with building experience and expertise and build with the materials that are there. The information is inside the coachee. Your curiosity allows the coachee to explore and discover. It opens a wider range of possibility because it is more flexible. Curiosity invites the coachee to look for solutions.

By finding the solutions in themselves—rather than in you (the coach or manager)—coachees become more resourceful. The effect of finding the answers is also very energizing because important learning takes place in the process of looking for and finding solutions. Curiosity generates the search, defines it, and directs it, but it is the exploring that creates learning. And it is the kind of learning that lasts, because it comes from within.

With questions that imply a correct or a purely factual answer, we search our inner files for the response that fits: the right answer. With curiosity, we have the experience of exploring, uncovering, digging around, considering, reflecting. This is the learning that leads to sustainable change and growth.

One of the clearest places to see the value of this approach is in the workplace. When managers ask from curiosity, it shifts responsibility to the employee; in the process employees become contributors, not just agents. This approach draws on their own resourcefulness and creativity, and they are more likely to own the results they achieve. Good news for managers: it also reduces dependency and builds a more proactive and accountable team.

The same effects happen in more traditional coach-coachee relationships, too, of course. This is the heart of transformation in the model.

Building the Relationship

Authentic curiosity is also a powerful builder of relationships—an aspect of curiosity that is very valuable in coaching. Imagine yourself at a dinner party seated next to a stranger who seems infinitely curious about you: your life, your work, your interests, what makes you tick, what ticks you off. This kind of curiosity is not only flattering but encouraging. It allows you to reveal a lot about yourself in an unchallenged way, so you build a connection effortlessly.

Now imagine the same dinner party and the same stranger asking questions, but this time the person is not simply curious. Instead, it's your prospective mother-in-law, and the questions seem to be part of an inquisition. The questions themselves might be exactly the same, but the context is vastly different. Curiosity builds relationships; interrogation builds defenses. In the coaching relationship, curiosity invites the coachee to search and reveal while permitting safe exploration.

Curiosity and curious questions are certainly not limited to a specific situation called *coaching*. Curiosity as a presence in an organization is a condition that creates deeper connection, promotes better personal relationships, and leads to better employee engagement. As such, it satisfies a key quest in every organization today.

Steering through Curiosity

The coach's question proposes a direction for looking, and the coachee's attention is naturally drawn in that direction. With each new question, the coach encourages additional looking along a path—or the coach shifts the path, allowing the curiosity to steer the looking. Being curious in coaching is two things: not being attached to a particular path or destination and yet always being intentional about seeking out meaning, uncovering important insight, and discovering learning for the coachee. It is not aimless meandering.

This would be a good time to emphasize that we are talking about curiosity for the sake of the coachee's discovery and decision making, not the coach's discovery and problem solving. This is an important distinction, and it is sometimes marked by a very fine line. Yes, of course it is important for coaches to gather information and background in order to understand the issue under discussion and the coachee's desires. But in practice, coaches usually need much less information than they think they do. This is especially true of background information. Coaches rarely need to know how things came to be. Coachees already know the background, and the coachee is the one who is making choices, taking action.

If there is a reason to be curious about the past or survey the background, it might be to look for patterns or themes that are useful in the present conversation. This is not so that coaches have a better understanding about what happened; it is so coachees have a better understanding of what they value, the way they make decisions, and how they persevere or sabotage themselves. That insight can then be applied to the current situation.

Developing the Talent

Like listening and intuition, curiosity is a talent. Some people are endowed with a stronger sense of curiosity than others. As with listening and intuition, curiosity can be developed through practice.

The first step is awareness—simply paying attention to being curious. We are so accustomed to feeling we have to know the answer before we ask the question that we sometimes find it nearly impossible to ask without knowing. In coaching, however, you have to learn to stop asking questions as the expert—with the intention of sorting, analyzing, and categorizing the information for later use—and simply ask out of curiosity.

Coachees know when the coach is asking a question with a "correct" answer in mind. They sense that they have two choices: either resist giving that answer or try to discern the answer the coach is looking for. When the question is asked out of curiosity, they will sense this, too. They will know they are being asked to find their own answers from within.

One technique for developing your curiosity is to use the phrase "I'm curious . . . " before asking a question. Notice how it changes the nature of the looking. Notice how it shifts the process of looking to the coachee but at the same time lowers the risk that usually accompanies coming up with the answer. Coachees seem more willing to say, "I don't know," and then answer anyway. With curiosity, there is both playfulness and an unconditional sense that the answer that emerges is always the right answer because it's the coachee's.

This doesn't mean it can't be challenged, however. It's a right answer because it's the coachee's, not the coach's, but it is also open to further coaching. When you ask the coachee, "How are you doing with making sales calls?" and the coachee says, "I'm satisfied with making four calls a day," you can still ask, "Your initial plan was for eight calls a day. What changed?"

Another application of curiosity is to notice the energy shifts in the coachee's responses using your Level III listening awareness. If your sensing radar picks up hesitation, be curious about that. If you pick up anger or resistance, ask about that. Be curious about a change in pace in the coachee's conversation—or a more energetic spirit, more jokes, more laughter. Use these clues as signals to pursue your curiosity and turn on your intuition.

How Curiosity Fits in Coaching

At some level, curiosity is one of those tools that are common to all helping professions. Curiosity is especially important in coaching because it taps into deeper sources of information. Asking questions for data will yield analysis, reasons, rationale, explanation. Asking questions out of curiosity will yield deeper—often more authentic—information about feelings and motivation. The information revealed through curiosity is likely to be less censored, less carefully crafted, messier. It will be more real.

The coach demonstrates curiosity in the very first meeting. Almost nothing is more engaging for prospective coachees than a coach's genuine curiosity about them, their values, what they find important, what does and doesn't work for them. Curiosity is always present in the ongoing coaching sessions, too, of course—in fact in any formal or informal coaching interaction. It is the means of uncovering new answers and new areas to explore, knowing that coachees know the answers. Coaches don't need to know. Their job is to be curious.

Sample Dialogue

COACH: I know you keep saying you want to exercise and lose weight—you just brought it up again—but week after week I notice you don't do anything about it. I'm curious. What's stopping you?

Coachee: Clearly, time is a big issue. You know what my schedule's been the last few months.

COACH: I know you're busy, but let's take a step back and really look at this. Maybe it's not that important?

Coachee: You mean I could just decide today that I don't care and I'd never have to go to the gym again?

COACH: That possibility certainly lit you up. What's that about?

Coachee: I hate going to the gym. I hate the smell. I hate all the comparison . . .

COACH: What is important to you?

Coachee: My health is important. My dad was overweight and out of shape. He was only sixty-eight when he died.

COACH: Imagine you are healthy and fit. What does that feel like?

Coachee: It feels great.

COACH: And what works for you?

Coachee: What would really work for me—at least, it did once before—is having a workout buddy, somebody to exercise with.

COACH: How can you make that happen?

Coachee: I'll bet I could find somebody at work who would be interested in exercising during the lunch hour. I could put a notice on the bulletin board.

Coaching Skills

The two skills in this section are ideal examples of the context created by curiosity. Both skills involve provocative, open-ended questions that send coachees in search of discovery. The skills reinforce the core of curiosity. This is not about gathering more information; it is about inviting coachees to look—not only with their minds, but with their hearts, souls, and intuition—into places that are familiar but that they may see with new eyes, and into places they may not have looked before.

Powerful Questions

A particular kind of curiosity takes the form of what we call *powerful questions*. Asking rather than telling is at the foundation of co-active coaching, and the powerful question is a cornerstone. You can see why when you understand what makes questions powerful to begin with. When a person asks you a question, especially a personal question, it sends you in a particular direction to find an answer.

Think of questions as points of a compass. Asking a powerful question is like sending the coachee not to a specific destination but in a direction filled with possible discoveries and mysteries. Powerful questions invite introspection, present additional solutions, and lead to greater creativity and insight. They invite coachees to look inside (*What do you really want?*) or into the future (*Look ahead six months. Standing there, what decisions would you make today?*). A powerful question is expansive and opens up further vistas for the coachee.

Powerful questions tend to stop people in their tracks, so there is often a sudden hush. Be sure to allow time for the coachee to reflect and then respond. There is a temptation to fill the momentary silence as if it were a void, or to assume that the coachee didn't understand the question. In fact, that silent moment may be full of thoughtful discovery. Just listen and wait. Coachees are accustomed to reporting what they know, what they have thought about already; they are not as accustomed to having people ask them really strong, provocative questions that send them into uncharted territory.

One way to tell that you are asking powerful questions is the thoughtful consideration coachees give to answering. It is possible, in fact, to conduct an entire coaching session with powerful questions. (The Co-Active Online Toolkit contains an extensive sample of powerful questions that will give you a sense of the form. *coactive.com/toolkit*)

Sample Dialogue

Coachee: I'm just not very happy at work.

COACH: What does that mean—"not very happy"?

Coachee: I'm bored and I don't feel like the work I do makes much of a difference.

COACH: Let's start with "bored." That's what you don't want.

What is it you do want?

Coachee: I want to wake up in the morning excited about the day. I want to be more creative. I miss that energy and the collaboration.

COACH: What else?

Coachee: I want to feel like my talents are being used and that my work means something—that I'm making a contribution.

COACH: How can you create that in your work now?

Coachee: I'm not sure. I guess I never thought of it as possible.

COACH: Give it a go. What's possible?

Using Powerful Questions

Powerful questions fit anywhere and everywhere in coaching—from the original discovery session to the last completion session between coach and coachee. To use powerful questions powerfully, the coach must be willing to intrude, a skill we discussed earlier. In some situations, you can't wait for an opening and need to wedge your way in.

Imagine this scenario: Your coachee is starting—once again—to complain about how impossible her workload is. She says it's unfair, there's never enough support, nobody cares, and she is helpless to change anything. You instantly recognize this recurring pattern as the unproductive recycling of the same old complaints, so when she pauses to take a breath, you ask, "What are you tolerating?" Or you ask, "What is the payoff for you in all of this?"

To ask powerful questions, the coach must be very curious and very courageous on the coachee's behalf. The coach needs to assume that the coachee has the wherewithal to handle even tough, direct questions.

Powerful Questions versus Dumb Questions

Sometimes the most powerful questions are the ones that sound the dumbest, or, if you prefer, simple and profound. They slide in under the radar. Coachees are well trained to handle the complex attack—they are practiced at offering explanations and rationalizations. The dumb question pierces through the fog like a laser.

Imagine this situation. Your coachee has a tightly constructed set of reasons that explain why moving forward with a decision is so complex, with lots of stories about all the interconnected factors that must be evaluated and considered, and even more stories about the lack of cooperation, the limited resources, the changing personnel, and . . . In the middle of this, you ask, "What do you really want?" Boom. You could have tested the rationale or looked for ways to test other perspectives or chipped away at the surface in some other way. But the simplest question, the dumb question, gets to the core.

Here are some other "dumb" questions:

- What does success look (or feel) like?
- What's next?
- What about that is important to you?
- What else?
- What did you learn?
- What will you do? When will you do it?
- Who do you need to be?

There are times when you may think the question is too dumb to ask—the answer is so obvious. Go ahead and ask it, and be open to being surprised. Even if you get the answer you expect, remember that the reason for asking is not so you can hear the answer; it is so the coachees can hear the answer and learn from it. By asking the dumb question, you allow coachees to hear the truth, the new discovery, or the lie they keep telling themselves. It's like underlining. Asking the questions reinforces the learning before coachees move on.

Not-So-Powerful Questions and Exceptions

When it comes to making questions powerful, the simpler and more direct, the better. Notice in our examples how short those questions are. Aim for seven words or less. A compound or complex question forces coachees to sort out the essence of the question before they can respond, and they may get lost trying to figure it out. The powerful question is powerful because it cuts through to the heart of the issue.

The closed-ended question creates a narrow tunnel that usually leads to an abrupt dead end, to a yes-or-no answer, or to data. There's not enough depth for further exploration, which is why we recommend avoiding closed-ended questions. Consider this question: "Is adventure important to you?" The answer could be "Yes," "No," "Very," or "Sometimes." It's like a quiz with multiple-choice options. Pick one. Compare it to this question: "Where do you want more adventure in your life?" That's the essay-style question.

This example also illustrates the exception with "yes-or-no" questions. Sometimes the coach is asking for clarification. In the first question, the coach is asking if adventure is a value. Sometimes there is a need to make sure the coach and the coachee are on the same page.

The "why" question is another example of a question that is often not particularly powerful because it invites the coachee to look for explanations or analyses. For example: "Why did you decide to move to Berlin?" "Why" questions often unintentionally put coachees on the defensive. They feel a need to explain or justify a decision or point of view. A more powerful question based on the same situation might be "What are you moving toward?" or "What values motivated this move to Berlin?"

We point out these tendencies not so you will make it a rule never to ask a "yes-or-no" or "why" question but so you will pay attention to the impact of the questions you ask. For example, the following "yes-or-no" and "why" questions could be powerful: "It's time to stop analyzing and act, isn't it?" and "Why would you say yes to him and break your promise to yourself?" Given the right context and a tone that matches that context, a "yes-or-no" or "why" question can have a dramatic effect on coachees, calling them to their own commitment.

Homework Inquiry

A homework inquiry is another special kind of question. In its phrasing, it can be identical to a powerful question. The difference is that the homework inquiry is often posed at the end of the coaching session and is meant to give coachees time for continued reflection and exploration.

For example, imagine that your coachee is struggling with money issues—and with working more and consequently having less family time—but she is hounded by a lifelong determination to be rich someday. So you present this question as the homework inquiry for the week: "What is it to be rich?" Or imagine that a manager in a coaching conversation is exploring a career path with a direct report. An inquiry might be, "What does leadership mean to you?"

A homework inquiry may also be completely unrelated to that session's issues. Because the direction of the question appears to be coming out of the blue, this kind of inquiry can produce unexpected and profound results. For example, at the end of the session, you ask the coachee, "What is your prevalent mood?" A week later you have a conversation with this coachee and discuss what the coachee learned from his exploration of prevalent mood. Then pose another inquiry: "How is this mood habitual, and how does it serve you?"

The homework inquiry is a question asked for the purpose of inviting introspection and reflection. As with any powerful question, there is no right answer. It is not a question that has a resolution. What sets the homework inquiry apart is the scale of exploration—the depth that is possible—and the time available to reflect on the question: several days, a week, or more.

Because there is a natural tendency to think that all questions should have their own right answers, you may need to remind the coachee that the goal of the inquiry is to be curious. In time, the inquiry leads to deeper understanding, new ways of looking at the issue, and more possibilities for action.

Here are some examples of homework inquiries:

- What is the underlying yearning?
- What are you here to do? To create?
- What are you resisting?
- What is it to be inspired?

To help coachees stick with the question, coaches may attach action to the inquiry. For example, a coachee might use the inquiry as a screensaver, or choose a key word from the inquiry as a log-on password for a week or two. Other action steps might be to process the question by writing in a journal, drawing pictures, talking to a friend, or going for a walk. You can build accountability into the inquiry by asking coachees to text, phone, or email their responses to you before the next session. The homework inquiry is a potent tool in coaching because it takes the coaching out of the session and integrates it into the coachee's life.

(For more examples, see the Co-Active Online Toolkit. *coactive .com/toolkit*)

Sample Dialogue

COACH: At the end of our last session, I gave you a question to ponder that could have many different answers at different levels.

Coachee: Right. "Where do you abandon yourself?"

COACH: How did that go?

Coachee: Well, at first I didn't see anything. And then I started realizing my helplessness around my calendar—how I never seem to have enough time because other people are filling up my calendar with appointments.

COACH: "Abandon yourself" in the sense of giving away your time to other people. What's it like when you give away your time?

Coachee: I noticed I had this habit of saying, "I can't do anything because my calendar is full"—until I finally realized that it's *my* calendar. I get to choose what I put in my calendar.

COACH: Where else do you abandon yourself?

Coachee: I also noticed it in my relationship. When my partner gets upset with me, I withdraw, disappear, or cave in. I'm getting better at taking a stand, but it's an old pattern.

COACH: What else did you discover with the question?

Coachee: Well, I just kept looking at it. I also noticed where other people give away their power.

COACH: Where was that?

Coachee: At a meeting last week. We had the divisional VP in to review forecasts, and some of the people were acting like nervous school kids in front of the principal. They just completely lost their self-confidence and authority. It was fascinating.

COACH: Was that true for you, too?

Coachee: More than I'd like to admit. I thought I was more beyond that than I guess I am.

COACH: Is there more?

Coachee: No, I think that covers it. Thanks.

COACH: So here's your homework inquiry for next week: Where do you take an uncompromising stand?

The Power of Being Curious

As a coach, your curiosity leads you to know your coachees from the inside out. You learn something . . . you become curious about that . . . it leads to more curiosity . . . and so it continues. Coachees in turn keep responding to your curiosity by going inside, too—looking for their own answers, trying to understand their internal world and the way they operate, what stirs them and what stops them. In time, you get to know their interior workings until, ultimately, you become their voice, asking the questions they themselves would ask. You, as the coach, are in a better position to ask these questions because you are not distracted by self-sabotaging talk, or history, or the opinions of colleagues and the feelings of loved ones, or anything else. The inquiries become more intriguing; the powerful questions become more potent. And in the process, coachees adopt some of the strengths of the coaching—as if they're building internal capabilities. Coachees learn what it's like to be curious and less judgmental about themselves.

Exercises

1. Curiosity

Spend thirty minutes in a coffee shop being curious about everyone in the place. Without actually talking to anyone at first, release your curiosity and pose the following questions to yourself: *I wonder where they are out of balance in their lives. I wonder what they value. I wonder what they are missing in their lives, what makes them laugh, where they have constructed self-imposed limits. What do they like about the day? What are their life dreams? What empowers them? What do they like about the people they're sitting with?*

At the end of the half hour, find someone you can spend a little more time with and actually ask that person the curious questions. As you ask the questions, be aware of what is happening with the other person. How does this person respond to you when you are curious? Then look at your own role in the conversation. What do you notice at Level I? At Level II? At Level III? Afterward, be curious about your own curiosity. What did you learn about being curious? What was easy? What was hard? What made it easy or hard? How could you be more curious? What would that give you?

2. Powerful Questions

One of the simplest ways to experience the power of powerful questions is also one of the most challenging. In this exercise, the goal is to have a 10-minute conversation with another person in which you are allowed to ask only powerful questions: no making statements, no summarizing, no offering advice or telling stories of your own, no drawing conclusions. Your role is to ask powerful questions and nothing more. (You may want to review the list of powerful questions in the Co-Active Online Toolkit. *coactive.com/toolkit*) Afterward, ask the person for feedback. What was it like when all you did was ask questions? Then tell the person what it was like for you to be confined to questions. What worked for you about that? What made it difficult?

3. Homework Inquiry

A homework inquiry is an open-ended, powerful question that helps coachees explore an important area of their lives for a period of time, usually a week or more. To do this exercise, start by reviewing the homework inquiries in the Co-Active Online Toolkit. Then go back to the list of 10 friends or acquaintances for whom you wrote meta-view statements at the end of chapter 3. Using the meta-view and what you know about the person, write a homework inquiry for each one.

CHAPTER 6

Forward and Deepen

The most visible outcome of coaching is also the primary reason coachees want coaching in the first place: action. Coachees want change; they want to see results. They want to move forward. It's also true that *action* will look very different for different coachees. For some coachees, it will mean achieving specific goals or performing at a higher level. For others, *action* means integrating new practices or firmly establishing habits. For still others, it will be paying attention to the more subjective quality of their lives. In whatever way coachees define *action*, it will be a focus in their coaching.

In co-active coaching, we say that a second outcome, which is complementary and just as important as action, is learning. What coachees learn along the way helps them make continuously better choices and, ultimately, makes them more competent and more resourceful in the areas they concentrate on in their coaching. In fact, it's this cycle of action and learning over time that leads to sustained and effective change. Coachees take action and learn, which leads to more action based on what they learned, and the cycle continues. Coaching is ideal for this process because the relationship is ongoing and is designed to focus on this interrelated pair. All of the coaching skills are used to forward the action and deepen the coachee's learning.

From the coachee's perspective, the emphasis in the previous sentence would be on the words *action* and *learning*. The coach, however, would focus on *forward* and *deepen*. Action and learning are what the coachee experiences. To forward and deepen is the job of the coach.

Imagine a coin. On one side you see the face of the coachee, and inscribed are the words that describe the coachee's focus: *to take action* and *learn from that action*. On the other side of the coin you see the face of the coach, or the leader in a coaching role. Here are inscribed the words that define the coach's role: *to forward the action and deepen the learning*. Each side has a different focus but a common bond. They are two aspects of the same thing, a relationship with a shared purpose.

The impact of this collaborative partnership is easy to see when we look at the more formal coach-coachee relationship. The coach in this scenario is a catalyst supporting the coachee in achieving certain results. Each of the roles is distinct. They have a designed alliance for the benefit of the coachee's agenda.

It may not be quite so obvious in those short, informal, coach-like conversations that a team leader has with a direct report, but the potential is there for valuable and lasting impact. For leaders, this approach accesses a mind-set that includes a focus on both results (action) and on growth (learning). This is, fundamentally, the role of leadership; both lenses are essential. Every initiative and every issue that arises is an opportunity for team members to learn in the process of taking action. At the same time, it is a way for leaders to develop their leadership eyesight: seeing those opportunities.

When there is equal value placed on forwarding the action and deepening the learning, coachees/employees develop strengths and become more valuable contributors. They also learn to be accountable for both the results they deliver and their learning. As leaders practice having their awareness on both action and learning, they hone their leadership abilities, and the organization benefits from a more engaged and effective culture.

The collaborative nature of the co-active model provides an ideal support structure for this. It creates working relationships and coaching relationships that flourish in the presence of four essential attributes: authenticity, connection, aliveness, and courage.

Authenticity

In rock climbing, the device that secures a rope is called an *anchor*. These ingenious devices are wedged into cracks and openings in the rock wall and can be removed later. They are temporary fixtures, but they are designed to hold a climber's weight, even if the climber falls. A coach is like that anchor. This anchor-coach makes it possible for coachees to take the risks they need to take in order to climb on in their lives. It's important that coachees be able to depend on that anchor and know that it is real and solid, that it is reliable and will hold.

In human terms, this means that you, as the coach, must be yourself, authentically, so that coachees can feel the honesty and integrity of who you are. You will be their model of what risk taking looks like, what it means to be real and honest. When you are authentically yourself and not playing the role of "professional coach," you create more relationship and more trust, and coachees will swing out more in their own lives. There are times when coachees really need to lean in to the coaching relationship; at that point, they want to lean in to a solid wall, one that is true all the way through, not a flimsy facade.

For leaders and managers, authenticity is key to building trust. In these times of rapid change and uncertainty, it's important for people to know what they can count on and *who* they can count on. Leadership authenticity forms a dependable foundation for effective collaboration.

Authenticity shows up in lots of ways. Personal style is one in particular. *Personal style* is simply your natural way of being with people, and if humor or eccentricity is an authentic part of your personal style, then you need to bring that into your coaching and leadership. Coaches sometimes think they have to be serious all the time. This is serious business, after all. Obviously it is important to take serious situations seriously and to behave professionally, but even so, there is plenty of room for lively engagement. Humor can lighten a situation at just the right time, making it possible for coachees to move forward.

Connection

Imagine there is an instrument that can measure the strength of the connection between coach and coachee. This invisible connection exists, like the radio waves used by mobile phones, and there are times when the emissions are strong and the communication is remarkably close, and times when the display on the phone would read "no signal" even though both people are talking.

Part of the coach's job is to establish, monitor, and maintain the strongest possible connection signal with coachees. This signal strength is especially important when coachees are moving into new or uncharted territory in their work or their lives. In our model, we call this a Level II awareness, or connection, and coaches monitor by listening at Level III and adjusting as necessary to maintain the connection.

There will be times in the coaching when the coach takes a risk with the coachee: to challenge or to tell the hard truth. If the connection is strong, there will be trust and relationship and a greater opportunity for success.

Aliveness

The *doing* of coaching is made up of all the skills and methodology. And then there is the *being* of coaching: the environment in which the coaching takes place. By *environment* we do not mean the physical environment, although that can play an important part in coaching. We are referring instead to a feeling in the atmosphere between coach and coachee: it feels very alive.

As a coach, your senses are alert, and you can feel that the coachee is alert as well. The emotional atmosphere might be almost anything: sad, serene, excited, angry. Alive does not necessarily mean enthusiastic, although that is one of the possible qualities. If you put the environment on a continuum, you might have words like *dead, dull, remote,* and *indifferent* on one end and *alive* on the other.

Note that there are times when *alive* will be very dramatic and times when it will be very quiet. Like a really great piece of music, the quiet can sometimes be incredibly alive—even intense—because it is in contrast with the dramatic movement. Coaches sometimes think that a coaching conversation should be smooth and polished, even smart. Of course it can be, but not at the expense of being alive. We have all been in conversations that were very alive even when the subject was uncomfortable. In order for coachees to leave their comfort zones, there will be times when the coaching will be very alive and very uncomfortable.

Courage

Speaking of uncomfortable, how far are you willing to go for the sake of your coachee's bold plans and purpose? How courageous are you willing to be on his or her behalf? Your willingness to be courageous will be a model, a mirror for your coachees. When you are courageous on their behalf, you demonstrate that you are as committed to their success as they are, on some days even more committed. At those times when coachees want to give in, you may need to courageously call them out of their fear or attitude of defeat.

This does not mean nagging, judging, or shaming them. It means speaking fiercely to the courageous part of your coachees while ignoring the part that is self-sabotaging. You do this not for the sake of your ego but for the sake of the coachee's life and growth. This is a commitment to be fearless—to care more about the coachee's agenda than about being liked or winning approval. It may mean taking big risks: risking the coachee's disapproval or anger, maybe even risking being fired. Fierce courage is a commitment to go to the edge with coachees.

Taking Charge

Your job as coach is to forward their action and deepen their learning. You do that by the choices you make as a coach: you choose to use this skill or that one; you choose a direction to take toward the coachee's fulfillment or balance or process. Coachees choose the agenda for their focus, but you choose the tools and manage the time and structure of the coaching session.

Coachees are responsible for their action and learning, and almost all of that action and learning takes place between, not during, coaching sessions. In the best coaching interactions, there is a dance between coach and coachee that has pace, range, ups and downs, ins and outs, and an overall flow that might look smooth or might look disconnected.

In the co-active coaching model, we emphasize that coachees have the answers and coaches are unattached; we emphasize that coachees are in charge of the agenda. We do want to be crystal clear, however, that the coach is primarily responsible for forwarding the action and deepening the learning. That's what it means to take charge of the coaching. It's not the specific *outcome* that coaches are responsible for; it's the process.

Coachees expect and depend on the coach to do this. You will still dance with the answers that coachees give and be willing to take the coaching in new directions that will move them forward and deeper. Ultimately, the coach takes charge for the sake of the coachee's movement.

That movement has purpose in it, purpose that matters to the coachee. The coach brings expertise in coaching as a way to help coachees stay in motion along their chosen path. If the coach is *not* taking charge of the coaching, then the coaching drifts or coaches simply default to the agenda du jour. Coachees come to coaching for a reason: for support or change in some important area of their life. Coaches have a responsibility to take charge of the coaching to optimize this unique opportunity and commitment. In an organizational setting, that coaching conversation about an upcoming deadline might not feel in the moment like a life-changing interaction, but it is in fact a contribution to a quality of life that values the best and what is possible for everyone involved.

Accountability

One of the defining qualities of coaching is that it creates accountability: a measuring tool for action and a means for reporting on learning. In a co-active approach, we believe *accountability* is simply this: Coachees give an account of their action and learning. There is no judgment, blame, or scolding. Coachees give an account of what they committed to: What were the results? What worked, and what didn't work? What would they do differently next time?

Accountability helps keep coachees on track as they plan and commit to action and as they learn from the action they take—or don't take in some cases. Accountability gives structure to the ongoing coaching. As coaches, we hold coachees accountable—not to see them perform or even to measure how well they perform, but to empower them in making the changes they want to make. Along the way, we celebrate their achievements and dig into the obstacles they encounter. Accountability is the fundamental structure that keeps the conversation going.

It is very important that coach and coachee have a mutual understanding of what the coachee will be accountable for, regardless of whether the action plan is very specific or very subjective. The basic questions to ask for clarifying commitments are simple and clear:

- What will you do?
- When will you do it? (*Or on what schedule, if it is a practice or an ongoing action.*)
- How will I know? (*Or ask how the coachee will track his or her progress and report back to you.*)

Even when accountability focuses on qualitative goals, there can still be specific accountability. For example, imagine that one of your coachees wants to focus on his value of creativity and another wants to be a more decisive manager. The accountability might take the form of a homework inquiry for daily journaling: "What does creativity add to my life?" or "What are the qualities of a decisive manager?" The accountability might be in the form of an end-of-the-day report to self: "Today I was creative when . . . " or "Today I was more decisive when . . . " or "Today I failed to be decisive when . . . " These same end-of-the-day reports might be sent to the coach by email along with notes about what the coachees are discovering.

Celebrating Failure

That may seem like an odd pairing of words, celebrating and *failure* side by side. And yet it may be one of the most important concepts in coaching. Fear of failing is the number one killer of grand plans and good ideas. More than a lack of knowledge or skill, more than the lack of a clear strategy or action plan, the biggest obstacle in the way of progress for coachees is the paralysis caused by the fear of failing.

Most of us learn early in life that failure is bad, even shameful. We learn to hide our failures, make excuses for them, or ignore them. Worse than that, we begin to stop taking risks; we become more cautious in order to avoid even the possibility of failing. We start to limit our choices to only those actions that have a high probability of success. And so our choices become limited, and our field of play becomes smaller. It doesn't have to be that way.

Failure is one of the fastest ways of learning. Ask any toddler. Small children do not stay up late at night reading the "how to walk" manual, learning the mechanics. They flop, fall, crawl, stand up, and flop and crawl some more. There are bumps along with steps and statistically more failure than success, but it never seems to dampen their enthusiasm. Similarly, in order to take the risks that will enable them to walk and run in their lives, coachees must be willing to flop, fall, and get back up and learn from the experience. Learning is the key here. Failing at any action, even failing to take action, is a rich learning opportunity. It is this learning opportunity that we celebrate and explore with coachees.

Action will lead to learning, but along the way, coachees may need to go through the land of failure. Here is an essential distinction that will help you pave the road through that territory: there is a difference between failing at something and being a failure. People are naturally creative, resourceful, and whole. They are not failures, even if they fail sometimes.

In fact, in order to make significant changes in their lives, coachees often have to go to the edge of their ability or capacity. Sometimes they go too far and fail; sometimes they don't go far enough and fail by missing the opportunity. Whether a person fails or succeeds, one of the underlying goals is always to look at the learning that results from the experience. That's why we believe that failing is valuable. It is something to honor in coachees because it requires courage and commitment to take the risk and to fail. Coachees will often learn more from what doesn't work than from what does work. And that is why we can enthusiastically put the words *celebrating* and *failure* side by side.

At the same time, we recognize that celebrating failure doesn't mean ignoring the disappointment that often accompanies it. Coachees may need a little time to absorb the bump before they can dig into the learning that is available there. Celebrating in this sense means having a reverence for, an appreciation of, the coachee's experience. We have a high regard for failing because so few people are willing to put themselves in that position. It's worth celebrating when it happens.

Calling Forth

Coaches, by their very nature, want to be helpful. They also want to be effective and successful and maybe even respected for their work, but at the core, they have a deep desire to help others. This is just as true for those in an informal coaching role. It's no wonder then that coaches jump at the chance to help coachees solve problems. That's the obvious way to be helpful: find the problem and solve it, make it disappear. Executives and managers learning to adopt a coaching approach with employees often confuse coaching as a softer, milder, indirect form of problem solving. The misunderstanding is understandable; it comes from old habits and expectations. Unfortunately, with this orientation, coaches—or managers as coaches—may become so focused on understanding the problem or the issue that they shift their attention from the coachee to the problem. In the long run, it is more helpful for coaches and managers to help coachees and employees to find their own way and make their own choices, to solve challenging problems and learn from the effort.

This puts the emphasis back on the person instead of the issue. As coaches or as managers in the role of coaches, we need to remember that we are not here merely to solve problems; we are here to help coachees or employees become more resourceful and more capable in their work and in their lives. Our job is to look for and call forth this inner strength and capacity from our coachees. We work with them to forward their action and deepen their learning in these everyday issues so that they can experience the satisfaction and reward of a bigger, more gratifying life. That's what it really means to be helpful.

If we are to call forth our coachees, we will need to call ourselves forth, too. There will be times when it is easier or more comfortable to hold back, to play it safe, to coast, to settle for less from our coachees. However, when we do that, we betray an unspoken trust. Those are the times when we as coaches need to find the courage to speak up, to insist or challenge or even demand, on behalf of our coachees that they live up to the capabilities they possess and that we see in them. We need to be ready to call forth the best in people, and sometimes that means we start with ourselves.

Coaching Skills

Each of the following skills is designed to forward the action and deepen the learning. The skills range in effect from tame and collaborative to powerful and assertive; all are designed to help coachees address the issues they face. The skillful coach will know when it is time to encourage the creative breadth of brainstorming and when it is time to light the fire for challenging.

Goal Setting

Without a specific goal, there can be endless drifting, a floating on the winds of this good idea and then that one. Goal setting gives coachees a specific direction and an action plan for making something real. Naturally the goals may shift over time as coachees make progress, but movement in the first place starts with setting their sights on a goal or an outcome.

Goal setting falls into two main categories: first, goals to reach at a specific time in the future and, second, ongoing goals. A goal for a specific time in the future might be "six completed projects by December 31" or "one completed project each month for the next six months." An example of an ongoing goal would be "working on new projects three hours a day, Monday through Thursday."

Part of your role as coach will be to help coachees create goals from their plans and intentions. Splitting the goal into manageable pieces is the first breakthrough for some coachees. Whereas once all they could see was the continent they had to cross, afterward they see many short excursions.

Helping coachees with the basics of goal setting can make a big difference in their success. The best goals are specific. They are measurable, or there is some way to track or monitor results. They are action oriented, even if the intention behind the action is qualitative. For example, the goal "think about moving to Alaska" will be strengthened by action. The coachee could buy a book about Alaska, find a poster that features Alaska, write in her journal about her memories of visiting Alaska, or talk to someone who lives there. And when there is a schedule involved, coachees are much more likely to take action.

Goal setting may seem so fundamental and obvious to you as a coach that you take it for granted. But even though it is fundamental, its importance and value should not be underestimated. As a coach, you need to have a clear understanding with coachees about how you and they will handle goal setting, looking for the ways that work best.

Sample Dialogue

Coaching provides a powerful structure for helping coachees get into action, stay in action, and learn from their action. Sometimes the action they crave is inaction.

COACH: I got your email. You took Wednesday afternoon off, just like you planned. That's great.

Coachee: It was weird.

COACH: The whole afternoon?

Coachee: Yeah. I almost checked my phone at one point—just an automatic habit—but I caught the impulse in time.

COACH: What did you learn?

Coachee: First, that those habits run *deep*. And second, that the world doesn't collapse if I'm gone for four hours.

COACH: Useful to know. What else?

Coachee: That I hired competent people—people I can trust.

COACH: Anything else?

Coachee: Micromanaging good people annoys them. And it takes up time I could be using to move the company into new areas. I've got to let go of control in some areas. I also learned I need downtime to recuperate. I'll burn out like a flash fire if I keep this up.

COACH: So what's the next step?

Coachee: Raise the bar?

COACH: Right. Now that you've had a taste, what's the stretch?

Coachee: I actually know what it is. I want to start planning a vacation for July.

COACH: Sort of takes your breath away, doesn't it? In order to make that happen, what will you do by next week?

Coachee: There's a travel agent in our building. I thought I'd stop by . . . and there's always the internet. I'll send you an email about what I discover.

Brainstorming

There are times when even good intentions and strong desire can be stalled by a simple shortage of ideas for action. Yes, of course coachees have the answers, as we have said, but sometimes it may be necessary to prime the pump. That's where the skill of brainstorming comes in. Brainstorming is a creative collaboration between coachee and coach with the sole purpose of generating ideas, possibilities, and options. The coachee will sort through the pile of ideas that are generated and pick the ones that have the most appeal.

There are a couple of ground rules that will make brainstorming work effectively. The first is that there are no bad ideas. Don't worry too much about practicality at the brainstorming stage. In fact, as coach, part of your role is to suggest out-of-the-box ideas and outrageous possibilities. Coachees tend to propose ideas they have already thought about or minor variations on those ideas. You make the process more creative and fun by stretching the net of possibilities. The second ground rule is that coaches should not be attached to their own good ideas and, above all, should not use brainstorming as camouflage for pitching their own solutions.

Brainstorming is generative, so look for ways to build on ideas, not just take turns adding one more idea to the pile. This can often make a commonplace suggestion into a more creative or personal one for coachees. For example, if your coachee suggests a half-day strategy meeting with key players, you might volley back with the idea of an off-site retreat and strategy meeting.

Sample Dialogue

Coachee: I'm a little stuck here. I haven't been on an actual date in fifteen years. I'd like to find a way to meet people, but I don't even know where to start. What do people do?

COACH: What would you like to do?

Coachee: I don't know. Have you got any ideas?

COACH: Want to do a little brainstorming?

Coachee: Sure. I'm desperate.

COACH: Okay. You go first.

Coachee: I used to go to bars when I was in college. I don't think I want to do that anymore.

COACH: So maybe you won't choose it—but it is an option. At this point, there are no bad ideas, just possibilities. Okay, the theme is social situations. What do you like to do for recreation? Skiing? Rollerblading?

Coachee: Hiking. Day hikes. Almost anything in nature.

COACH: Great. You could join a hiking club, or you could start one for singles. What's another option?

Coachee: One of those computer dating services, I suppose.

COACH: OK. How about volunteer work? You place a high value on community service. What would be an area where you might volunteer your time?

Coachee: The school where my kids go. I would like to be more involved with them.

COACH: What other values would you like to tap into as you create opportunities to meet people? You mentioned nature . . . and we talked about community service . . .

Coachee: When you said *nature*, that hit a chord. I think there are possibilities there.

Requesting

Over and over, we've emphasized that this is the coachee's agenda—that the coachee is resourceful, that the coachee knows the answers or knows where to find them. Still, it will be appropriate at times for you, the coach, to request certain actions. Based on your training, your experience, and your knowledge of your coachees, you'll have a sense—usually based on actions coachees are already considering—of what direction they might take for maximum learning. You simply put the action into the form of a request so that the action is clear and the coachee is accountable.

For example, imagine that you and your coachee are working on family finances and ways of creating order. You might say to your coachee, "This week, my request is that you create a detailed monthly budget for personal and household expenses. Will you do that?" Note that the language of a request takes a somewhat specific form: there is the request itself stated in a way that is specific and measurable (the coachee can actually be accountable for something), and there is the question at the end that asks for commitment. This is more powerful than simply asking a coachee to work on finances this week. The language draws a line in the sand and puts the coachee on notice that this is important business. In time, using this format, coachees learn that taking on a request is an act of personal commitment, not just acceptance of an assignment from their coach.

The key to making a successful request is to not be attached to it. The moment you become attached to the brilliance of your own idea and start thinking it's the right way for the coachee to get results, it's your agenda, not the coachee's. With a request, there are always three viable responses: yes, no, or a counteroffer. The coachee can agree to your request, turn down your request, or negotiate for something else. If your idea is turned down, feel free to defend it a little. You might explain why you think it works and the value it would have. Maybe the coachee didn't understand completely the first time. You might even probe to make sure that the "no" was not simply a fear reaction.

If the coachee turns down your request, look for the counteroffer. You might ask, "What will you do?" As far as you, the coach, are concerned, the whole point is some form of action or learning—and as long as that happens, it doesn't matter who comes up with the action plan.

The art of requesting, by the way, is as much a life skill as it is a coaching skill or co-active relationship skill. In organizations with the fast pace of work life and enormous pressure to get things done, people often choose the "easier" path: they swallow the complaint, tolerate the situation, and move on. However, over time that irritation becomes a growing toxin, poisoning the atmosphere. In many cases, a simple request early on can prevent that suffering sequence.

Sample Dialogues

Coach Practitioner and Coachee

Coachee: One more thing. We've talked about my lack of discipline around exercise . . . even though I say it's important.

COACH: What's up?

Coachee: I think I've found a motivation.

COACH: What's that?

Coachee: I suppose I'm like everyone else with a 10-year reunion. I'd love to lose about 10 pounds.

COACH: How's your workout program going?

Coachee: I get to the fitness center about once a week. I know it's not enough.

COACH: As I recall, swimming is your exercise of choice. Is that right?

Coachee: Right. I was on the swim team one year.

COACH: Okay. Let's make this simple. My request is that you swim a minimum of 30 minutes four times a week. Will you do that?

Coachee: You know what? I'd rather do 40 minutes three times a week. That saves me one trip, and it's the same amount of time.

COACH: How do you want to be accountable?

Coachee: I'll make it a weekly check-in statistic—right when we start.

Manager and Direct Report

MANAGER: How's it going with the two new graphic designers?

Direct Report: It's going . . . OK.

MANAGER: You don't sound very convincing.

Direct Report: They're both excellent at what they do.

MANAGER: And? I sense there's more here.

Direct Report: I don't want to stifle their creativity, but they have a tendency to go a little crazy with their ideas, and they tend to feed off each other.

MANAGER: What's the impact of that?

Direct Report: We're running behind schedule, and frankly we're losing continuity in the way the material needs to be presented. Clients are noticing.

MANAGER: What's the opportunity for you in this?

Direct Report: Giving feedback. Learning to give supportive but clear direction. I want to get more comfortable with that.

MANAGER: I have a request . . . with the usual "yes," "no," or "counteroffer."

Direct Report: OK.

MANAGER: How about morning stand-up feedback meetings—10 or 15 minutes with each of them. Make some notes in advance so you're prepared.

Direct Report: I can do that. One change, though. I think I'll do them both together—maybe they'll hold each other accountable for the feedback.

Challenging

A challenge asks coachees to extend themselves beyond their self-imposed limits—way out to the edge of improbability. If the challenge is powerful enough, it should cause coachees to sit up straight and exclaim, "No way." If that's the response, then you know you're in the right territory. Your idea of their potential is much bigger than the picture they hold of themselves. Coachees often respond with a dual reaction: exasperation when confronted with the enormity of your challenge but also a sense of being emboldened because someone believes in them that much. Most coachees will flatly turn down your challenge but then make a counteroffer—at a level higher than anything they would have considered on their own initiative.

Imagine working with a coachee whose particular form of self-sabotage is being too agreeable, taking on too much. This inability to maintain reasonable boundaries is creating great stress; it's a pattern this coachee wants to break. At some point in the coaching conversation, you challenge your coachee: "I challenge you to say *no* 30 times a day this week." Your coachee counters: "No way. That's impossible. I'd be fired in a week!" You say, "Well, that's your first *no*. Just 29 to go." Your coachee counters: I'll do 10 a day, but that's my limit." You say, "Fifteen." Your coachee agrees. So instead of talking more about how hard it is and the consequences of saying *yes* when a *no* is called for, your coachee will be practicing an affirming behavior 15 times a day. Such is the power of the challenge.

Sample Dialogue

> **Coachee:** It's like a dark cloud that's been hanging over me for the last six months!

> **COACH:** The way you've talked about it, it feels like much more than a cloud. You've been in this dark mood for weeks. You said you felt listless and you're not eating well . . . all because of this manuscript you have to finish.

> **Coachee:** Research paper. Actually, the research is done. All I need to do is write it up.

> **COACH:** When will you get it done?

> **Coachee:** At this rate, I don't know.

> **COACH:** How many hours will it take? What's your best estimate?

> **Coachee:** Hard to say. Maybe 30 hours—a little more, a little less.

> **COACH:** I have a challenge for you. My challenge is that you finish the paper before we talk next week.

> **Coachee:** Next week? That's crazy!

> **COACH:** Could you do it in a week?

> **Coachee:** Well, yeah. If that's all I did.

> **COACH:** What will you do?

> **Coachee:** I'll work on a rough draft.

> **COACH:** "Work on . . . ?" What does that mean exactly?

> **Coachee:** OK, I'll have a draft finished—it may have a few holes.

Putting Structures to Work

We know that accountability in the coaching relationship is a structure. It's a means by which we create focus and discipline. In fact, a structure is any device that reminds coachees to be in action in the areas they have committed to. Structures intervene in everyday life, they stand out, they require attention, they are devices to keep coachees on track. Structures come in a myriad of forms. Setting an alarm to wake up is a simple example of a structure—it reminds you what time it is: time to get up! There is an endless variety of creative ways to sharpen focus and get into action.

Different structures appeal to different senses. Some are tactile: wearing that power suit to the board meeting. Some are visual: a picture on the office desk of a dream home or vacation destination. Structures can be auditory: a special piece of music as a personal soundtrack to help complete a project or enjoy a workout.

Coachees make commitments to be in action, and often everyday life gets in the way. The familiar routine of life, the demands of family and job, even the coachee's own resistance to change can derail good intentions and personal promises. The power of the structure is that it reminds coachees and recalls them to their commitment.

Here are some other examples of ways to create structures:

- Create a special screen saver with a theme line or visual image.
- Post notes around the office or home with affirmations or reminders.
- Track daily or weekly progress toward major goals on a wall chart.
- Listen to a meditation tape or an audio book or create an audio file of your own personal motivation.
- Choose a particular piece of clothing—magic armor—when making sales calls.
- Light a candle or burn incense.
- Put a special reminder in your pocket, something like a small stone or toy.
- Change the lighting in the room by making it brighter or dimmer, or change the light's color.
- Create deadlines, such as inviting people to your house for a party so that you will finish painting a room or do some housecleaning.
- Establish creative consequences or rewards.

Structures are a way of sustaining the action and learning in the time between coaching sessions. Each coachee will be somewhat more responsive in different sense areas. Experiment with structures to find out what works, and keep playing with them. The key word here is *play*. The reason for the structure is to provide discipline and focus in an area where it may be difficult for coachees to stay on track. By making structures playful, you increase the chances that coachees will follow through.

Exercises

1. Requesting

Look behind any complaint and you will almost always find a request that could have been made instead. In a restaurant, if you've got a complaint about the draft blowing down on you from the overhead air conditioner, you can sit with your complaint or you can make a request. When an appropriate request is made, action often happens, and that takes care of the complaint.

So here's the exercise: Make a list of 25 complaints in your life—things that just aren't going your way. They don't have to be reasonable. If you have a complaint about the weather, write it down. Acts of God are not off-limits for complaints or requests.

When you have your list of 25 complaints, compose a request that addresses each complaint. Target your request to a specific person whenever possible, someone who has the power and the ability to do something about your request. Then, for as many of the complaints as possible on your list, actually follow through and make the request. And remember, there are always three legitimate responses to your request: yes, no, or a counteroffer.

2. Challenging

Go back once again to the meta-view list of 10 friends or colleagues you made in chapter 3. Your goal in this exercise is to write a challenge for each person, addressing each one's meta-view in a way that dramatically raises the bar. You are trying for action steps that will move these people forward and provide extraordinary learning. Make sure you come up with true challenges—situations that ask them to go further than you know they will go—so that they end up making significant counteroffers.

3. Structures

Here is a simple and somewhat typical situation: Your coachee is much too busy to keep his office clean, yet the chaos that results is seriously distracting him. It has reached the point of no return. Something must be done. Your job is to come up with 10 structures that will help this person stay in action to get his office orderly and organized. Alternately, think about an area in your own life that could benefit from focus. Come up with 10 structures for yourself that you could use to remind you of the importance of this situation.

The bottom line: People who come to coaching don't come because they don't have enough to do. They often come because they have SO MUCH to do and want to have the support to focus on what is important out of all the options they are handling. Everyone at work is in a similar situation. They have a load of requirements and expectations to sort through, and sometimes the really important things they want to accomplish get lost in the shuffle. Structures provide a focus—they are a flashing light in a very busy environment.

CHAPTER 7

Self-Management

This is the picture we continue to hold as the ideal for any coaching interaction: *You and your coachee, 100 percent connected. You, as coach, listening intently at Level II, following, tracking. And listening at Level III, aware, sensing—open to your intuition as you let the conversation flow through you and around you. It's as if you and the coachee are in a bubble, a safe chamber that isolates the two of you from the distractions of the outside world.* That's the ideal. But sometimes, in the midst of this intense, engaged conversation, the phone rings. Or a metaphorical bell goes off in your mind: a thought, a feeling. Suddenly, that protective zone evaporates. You disengage, detoured to that other thought or feeling. You are disconnected from your coachee.

It happens. In any given conversation with a coachee, it may happen many times. Something in what your coachee says triggers a distracting thought or reaction in you or reminds you of an experience in your own life, a strong memory. These are very human reactions that will cause you to go away in your mind and feelings, even if it is only temporary.

It could be a completely unrelated thought dropping out of the blue: you suddenly remember you have forgotten to make dinner reservations at the restaurant after promising you would handle it. The coaching itself might create a distraction, such as a moment of special brilliance or a feeling that you're handling the coaching badly and your attention is on your judgment, not on the coachee. Or you may be distracted by something that happens in the environment: dogs barking, sirens sounding, a storm outside. It might be something only you notice—the window is open and the rain is coming in, soaking a pile of important papers.

Naturally, you want to create an environment and conditions that minimize the chances of these sorts of distractions, but they will happen from time to time. The context of self-management is a combination of self-awareness and the skill of recovery. It is an awareness of yourself, an ability to notice where you are or where you have gone in relationship with your coachee, and it is about the ability to get back, to reconnect.

Self-management is also about getting connected and engaged in the first place. This is particularly challenging in an organizational setting, where most coaching opportunities for leaders and managers are not scheduled events. They often happen spontaneously or without a formal setup that defines the meeting as a specific coaching interaction. Think about that 15-minute conversation between manager and direct report that takes place after the staff meeting finishes. It wasn't planned in advance, but it might be the most important coaching opportunity of the day.

Here's the summary: In a co-active relationship, self-management is an expression of your total commitment to that other person; it's about creating the optimum one-to-one connection in the moment, which is why it holds an important place in the co-active contexts. One hundred percent connected is the ideal. Self-management is what we do as coaches or leaders to engage or recover when conditions create less than 100 percent connection.

Bumped Off Course

Coachees are human—which is another way of saying they are somewhat unpredictable. One of the most common situations involving self-management is when a coaching session takes surprising twists and turns or the coachee's primary coaching focus changes dramatically from session to session. This ability to engage with coachees wherever they are when they show up for coaching is so essential to being an effective co-active coach that we have made it one of the four cornerstones: the ability to dance in this moment. Agility in the dance requires a high level of self-awareness and self-management.

The context of self-management also involves knowing the difference between simply wandering along wherever the coachee leads, and holding a particular focus with the coachee. Asking yourself, "Are we still on track here?" may take you away from the conversation momentarily, as if an observer in you is watching the conversation unfold. And yet there are times when that momentary pause—a brief stepping back to monitor what's happening—is important in order to keep the coaching on track and stay connected.

It gets trickier when you, as the coach, are distracted by the content of the coaching conversation or even the presenting issue itself. You may find yourself suddenly up to your ears in technical details that are hard to follow, or trying to decode the coachee's work jargon and acronyms. You may have reservations about a plan of action your coachee wants to take. That's a distraction. In fact, you may not always agree with your coachees' plans, and yet the self-management course is to honor their action as theirs: theirs to work with, to change as necessary, to fail at completely or succeed at gloriously, and to learn from, always.

There are also times when it is appropriate to say something. For the sake of your own integrity, you may decide it's important to share your reservations but with the caveat that you are offering your own experience and opinion, not "the right answer."

For managers, there is a very natural instinct to want to offer advice or jump in to help fix things. Holding back can be a real self-management challenge. But when you see that this is an opportunity for a *coaching* conversation, the context justifies your restraint. Rest assured there will be other conversations where your expertise or advice are naturally and obviously called for.

In any coaching exchange, tracking the content of the conversation and the direction it's flowing is an important example of self-management. But self-management has a very personal aspect for coaches, too. Coaches are also human; they are somewhat unpredictable and sometimes susceptible to emotion. They are prone to react, sometimes abruptly. It could be the subject matter under discussion that sparks a reaction or even a single word. Your coachee may use language you find objectionable, or say something disparaging about someone you admire or a coworker—someone on your team. It's inevitable that out of all the material coachees bring to you, something at some point will trigger your own pet peeves, or your personal standards or sensibilities will bump up against a coachee's comments.

In that "bump," you are affected. You might become judgmental, defensive, offended, or simply annoyed. The reactions vary widely, but the condition is best known as being "hooked." It's as if, in that moment, a very large hook had been inserted in you and yanked. There you are, lost in your own thoughts and opinions at Level I; you are no longer focused on your coachee.

It can happen when you least expect it. Imagine that you have a coachee who has been practicing the skill of saying no: no to working long overtime hours without being compensated, no to unhealthy snacks that deplete his energy, no to coworkers who take up valuable time with trivial chitchat, no to a particularly toxic relationship. Progress on this commitment has been inconsistent, but lately he seems to be moving forward.

In today's coaching session, it all comes apart: he has agreed to work overtime this weekend; he has binged every afternoon on bad food; and he's decided to give that dysfunctional relationship one more chance. You would like to be calm, compassionate, and patient, but you have seen this backsliding one time too many. You can also clearly see the impact and the price he pays for caving in. It makes you crazy that he can't see it for himself or—worse—that he can see it and is choosing this self-sabotaging behavior anyway. In that disheartening moment, you can feel the steam building under your collar, your heart beating faster. You've really had it with this crap!

Whoa! Even if this anger comes from the best possible intentions and your caring for this coachee, in this minute the steam, the frustration, the temper are in danger of taking you away, breaking the connection between coach and coachee.

The opposite can also happen. Imagine that you have been working with a coachee for three months, and in that time, she is no closer to her goals today than on the day you two started your coaching relationship. Nothing of consequence has happened. Here you are again. She is droning on, repeating the same reasons why she can't take action. You've tried every technique and trick you can think of, but it is like pushing water up a straw.

Today your own self-judgment is having a field day with your "inadequate coaching." The conclusion? You have failed; you are in over your head; you don't have the skills; you have done nothing in three months to help this deserving soul who is counting on you. Now you don't even have the courage to admit it and assist her in getting the help she needs and deserves from someone more qualified. Meanwhile, as you are having this self-flagellating internal conversation, your coachee is floundering, wondering where you have gone.

The signals are there to see. When you find yourself trapped in self-analysis—defending, judging, feeling annoyed—the alarm bells should be going off. When you find that you are hooked or caught up in a personal emotional reaction, you are no longer with your coachee; you are with your own Level I reactions, thoughts, and feelings. You are trapped in a cage, racing inside that little exercise wheel, going nowhere. You need to find your way back to your coachee and reconnect.

This concern is often exaggerated in leaders and managers, and it is a main reason they don't engage in coaching conversations. They are afraid they'll do it wrong ("I haven't had enough training") or afraid they'll harm someone ("I'm not a therapist"). Beliefs like that are a crippling Level I narrative when the fact is that a curious, engaged, and co-created conversation is simply about two people in a dialogue with a common purpose. It can be quite normal.

Forbidden Territory

Self-management also includes where you stop or hold back in your coaching. It would be wonderful if all great coaching could happen within the coach's comfort zone. It doesn't. There are places coaches don't want to go, where they are unsure of themselves or afraid it will get messy.

Maybe, in coaching, you sometimes avoid telling the hard truth because you don't want to make waves or upset coachees—especially if they become upset with you. Maybe you hold back because you don't want to lose a coachee or you're afraid of repercussions in the organization. Coaches may hold back because they don't want to risk offending, but what they risk instead is a less resourceful life for their coachees or simply weak, but polite, chitchat. Is it possible that a coachee will get upset and quit? Yes, it's possible. If the coaching conversation isn't stirring, it's stagnant—missing the aliveness we described earlier.

The irony is, the areas where you feel uncomfortable—that road you don't want to go down—could be the very road this coachee needs to travel. And by the way, it could be a road that the coachee might be well-equipped to handle, even if you aren't.

Take a hard look at the areas in your own life where you get tangled up—where you see a pattern of historical trouble for yourself. Chances are, those are the same areas you are unwilling to probe in the coaching sessions. For you, they are blind spots, created out of self-protection. They are probably invisible to you most of the time. Maybe one day you'll work through what holds you back in your life and be free of those hesitations, but you can't wait for that to happen before you explore those places with your coachees.

Maybe loneliness is unbearable for you, so when a coachee raises the issue of loneliness, you quickly but unconsciously shift the coaching in a different direction and find something else that is easier to talk about. Because of the emotional charge the issue has for you, you don't do the kind of exploration that would benefit your coachee. Or maybe the issue involves taking a stand and speaking the truth to those in authority, or awkwardness around money or intimacy. Delving into these areas may be crucial to your coachees' action and learning. Self-management is about recognizing that these are uncomfortable issues for you but then exploring them anyway for the sake of your coachee. You must be willing to coach outside your comfort zone.

Self-Judgment and Good Judgment

It is probably safe to say that, as a group, coaches place a high value on learning and growth—their own as well as that of their coachees and the other people in their life. Consequently, coaches often have a highly developed habit of self-analysis, which can sometimes manifest as unwarranted self-judgment.

Self-management is about recognizing the self-judgment going on inside your brain and knowing the difference between constructive analysis and self-destructive chatter. The key for you as a coach is the same key you give your coachees. First, notice. Make sure you record it well in your mind. What was the criticism or observation, precisely? Be clear, be descriptive, be attentive to the experience. Then ask yourself a couple of questions: *What is the truth in that for me? What's in that for me to learn?* Something happened in there that hooked you or caused a reaction, and it's worth paying attention to it.

Before deciding on the worst possible interpretation of the experience, allow yourself some room to reflect. Obviously this reflection is something you will undertake outside the coaching session, on your own with a colleague, or with your own coach. It's important to recognize that these disruptive experiences are part of learning and growing stronger as a coach and a person. The more adept you become at recognizing and working with your own self-judgment, the more you'll be able to help coachees work with theirs.

Self-management is also about knowing when you really are in over your head. When that realization strikes, be gentle with yourself. In such a situation, the most constructive thing you can do for the coachee—and for yourself, by the way—is to refer him or her to another coach or another resource for help. This coachee may be better off with a career counselor or a therapist or a more detached coach. Sometimes the chemistry is not right—there isn't a good fit and you don't see that until you work together.

For managers working with team members, a comparable self-management situation would be one where using a coaching approach is simply not working in that relationship in spite of your best efforts. That could be true for more reasons than we have room to enumerate here. In the context of self-management, the lesson is to be aware. Don't force, don't judge, and look for alternatives for this employee.

A heightened awareness of self-management for managers has other benefits, too. Not only are they able to be more present in conversations generally, but they also become more aware of default patterns that often get in their way. The practice of self-management provides an opportunity for self-discovery about reactive habits, and that awareness can lead to more creative responses.

Practices

Disconnected? Say So

Let's be honest. Despite your best intentions to always be present and engaged, you will disconnect from your coachee from time to time. It can happen for many reasons—some significant, some trivial. You happen to glance at your desk and notice an important appointment on your calendar you'd forgotten about . . . somebody is knocking on the door

. . . something your coachee just said reminded you of a very annoying conversation with a coworker. In that moment of disconnect, one of the most powerful things you can do is to admit it: "I'm sorry; I just went blank for a moment. Would you repeat what you just said? I missed that."

Admitting that you disappeared actually creates trust and reaffirms your commitment to your coachee. You may think you hide your vanishing act from coachees, but they often sense your disappearance even if they don't say so. More than that, you model the veracity that builds a strong relationship between you and your coachees. Coachees respect your honesty about what happened—that you didn't try to cover it up or pretend you were paying attention when you clearly weren't—and they see your admission as a way of saying that you are really committed to them.

Be Ready

This is about being prepared for the upcoming coaching session in the usual ways you would prepare for any important conversation. It could be as simple as reviewing your notes from the most recent coaching session. More than that, in order to be present and ready, many coaches have a ritual they use before the appointment. Rather than jump right from one multitasking moment to the next you could give yourself a few minutes of quiet reflection, recalling to mind your intent or purpose. It is a structure for orienting yourself to the coaching—preparing for coachees in physical, emotional, mental, and even spiritual ways.

As a self-management practice, this kind of preparation is especially important when your personal life is getting the best of you. You are a human being as well as a coach. Periodically, things will happen that can cause you to focus your attention on yourself rather than on the coachee. Let's say you get stuck in traffic on your way to the office. You feel rushed, harried, and anxious about being on time. In situations like this, you need to clear your feelings and get your feet on the ground before speaking with your coachee so that you can concentrate fully on the coachee and not on your troubles or residual stress.

Apart from the everyday annoyances that may knock you off balance before a coaching call, there is also the punch in the solar plexus. Maybe you just received bad news about a friend: the biopsy is back, and the lump is cancer. Or you just walked out on a devastating argument with your partner over an issue you thought was settled.

Under those circumstances it can be very challenging to find a way to be fully present for your coachees. You might check in with a colleague or your own coach, but recovering to a personal and professional state of mind in that case is not easy. Sometimes it's not even possible, and you need to tell coachees that you have to reschedule their appointments. The questions for any coach or any manager about to step into a coaching role are simple but essential: *Are you ready? Or can you be ready?* Yes, you need to be strong for your coachees. Gritting your teeth and persevering when the going is tough is admirable—but only up to a point. Self-management is about knowing where that point is.

Opinions and Advice

The Manager's Dilemma

For leaders and managers, this is a common self-management moment: You have an employee with an issue to solve, or a challenging problem to untangle. You work in a pressure-packed world with a relentless drive to get results, move projects forward, make decisions. You're aware that the clock is ticking.

You are a firm believer in coaching as an essential leadership competency and as a tool for growing competence on the team. You're committed to coaching your direct reports; you've seen the value. And yet—sometimes the urge to solve the problem or give advice is almost overwhelming. This is definitely a self-management moment. You're on the spot trying to figure out both the nature of the issue and how to be most helpful. You're asking yourself, *Who am I in this moment? Am I the boss? The subject matter expert? Confidante? Coach?*

Ultimately, the question to answer as manager is, *What will best serve this employee—now and in the future?* Your answer to that question must consider a number of things: the employee's development, the growth of the team, and the ability of the team to perform at a higher level tomorrow than it does today. The approach to the presenting opportunity is a balance of *What is there to learn here?* as well as *What is there to fix?* In the end, you will need to trust your instincts—and be aware of your default or impulse reaction. Sometimes the most efficient, expedient, and correct response is not another powerful coaching question; it's an experience-tested solution. That's the self-management context.

The Coach's Dilemma

We continue to emphasize that people are naturally creative, resourceful, and whole and that they do have the answers or know how to find them. Still, at times it may seem pointless to withhold your knowledge or experience when it is clearly relevant and could spare coachees time, money, effort, and anxiety. Coachees may not look to you for expertise in the same way an employee might look for answers from his or her manager, but there are those times when—even without being asked—you see you have something to contribute.

Here's the key: as long as you are conscientious about framing the conversation as your experience and encouraging coachees to find their own best way while exploring a number of alternative pathways, your experience will be seen as one more potential course of action and not the "expert's" way. In short, don't make it a rule that you will never share an opinion or a bit of advice. Self-management is a context of discretion, always in the coachee's best interests.

This discretion also extends to sharing your personal story. Most of the time, it's best to keep your personal story to yourself. As a coach, you have a different relationship with your coachees than you would have if you were their friend. Your relationship in a coaching session is different even from those that coachees have with coworkers, colleagues, or managers.

The attention in the coaching session is directed to coachees and their lives and agendas. In almost all cases, it is inappropriate and a waste of the coachee's time for you to share your personal story. We say "in almost all cases" quite intentionally, because there may be times when a little of your story will be important in building trust and relationship with a coachee. The fact that you are human, not just an anonymous, impersonal resource, will contribute toward building a strong, co-active relationship.

The key word there is *relationship*. We believe that strong relationship creates trust, safety, and openness, and it is this deeper relationship that allows coachees to take the bigger risks they need to take in order to make the boldest, life-giving choices or develop their talents as team contributors. But as you can see, it leaves room for interpretation and discretion. Ultimately, in the co-active model, the decision hangs on what will be best for the coachee in the long run.

The Benefits for Coachees

We have described the context of self-management here primarily from the point of view of the impact on the coach, but a coach's developed sense of self-management benefits coachees, too. As the coach models the attributes of self-management, coachees see the impact; they learn to become more aware of what is happening in the moment, noticing when they have disconnected. They learn to speak up about what is true even if it might be awkward, and they learn to recover, to reconnect to the relationship. This benefit ripples out beyond their coaching sessions and into their lives, creating stronger relationship.

In fact, just as coachees develop better listening skills or learn to trust their intuition more as a result of their immersion in coaching, coachees also learn about self-management in their lives. Coachees learn to be more aware of their own inner experience, especially situations where they habitually get hooked or derailed. Training coachees in this context of self-management can help them be aware of and quicker to recognize these situations, and they learn to be more resourceful.

Coaching Skills

A number of coaching skills are generally associated with self-management. These skills underscore the dynamics in the relationship and help coach and coachee maintain their individual strengths.

Recovery

Clearly, the most obvious skill for the context of self-management is the skill of recovery: the ability to notice the disruption or disconnection and to reconnect. For the coach, the disconnect could simply be a case of confusion—losing the thread of the coachee's conversation—or it could be a much stronger emotional reaction to the subject at hand or something the coachee said. There are three parts to the skill: noticing, naming, and reconnecting.

Notice It

This awareness step is crucial. It is not necessary to know exactly what happened, and it is completely unnecessary to know why or what caused it—at least in the moment. It is important to simply notice the gap, the shift, the disconnect.

Name It

Describe what just happened: "I got lost," or "I was distracted for a minute." Sharing this awareness with your coachee is optional, but we encourage it so that your coachee is clued in to where you are. It is amazing how quickly the coaching can get back on track simply by realigning with the coachee.

Reconnect

Each person will have a different tactic for connecting, and each situation may require a different process. Fundamentally, it is the process of turning your attention back over to your coachee—that Level II connection, engaged and present.

Asking Permission

One of the most important techniques the coach uses to remind coachees that they are in charge of the coaching direction is to ask permission: "May we work with this issue?" "Can I tell you what I see?" "Would you like some feedback on that?" When the coach asks permission, it demonstrates that coachees have power in the relationship. It demonstrates, too, that the coach knows the limits of his or her power in the relationship.

Asking permission is a sign of self-management on the coach's part, and it allows coachees to take responsibility for managing the relationship and their work. Coachees are honored when you ask permission; their boundaries are respected. This is especially important when the issue you'd like to work on is unusually intimate or may make coachees uncomfortable: "May I tell you what I see about the way you've been handling this?"

Sample Dialogue

Coachee: I guess I realized that the plan I agreed to just wasn't going to work. I had to improvise on the spot . . . tap dance my way through it. It was like old times, making it up as I went along.

COACH: First of all, there's nothing sacred about the plans we work out. You still get to choose the best course of action for you. I trust that you know what's right and that you'll move forward and learn from whatever you decide to do. So what did you decide?

Coachee: That's basically what I did. I took action. Just a different course of action.

COACH: Before we move on, I'd like your permission to give you some feedback on the way you handled the situation—based on what you've said in the past. Would that be okay?

Coachee: I have a feeling I may not like all of what I hear. But yes, of course. If there's a chance to learn something valuable, I'm all ears.

Bottom-Lining

There are times when a coachee's telling of his or her story begins to expand and take over the coaching session. Or times when the coachee starts wandering tangentially through story after story. Sometimes it's the coachee's style of conversing; many times it's a way of unconsciously avoiding difficult or direct conversation. Bottom-lining is the skill of getting to the point and asking the coachee to get to the point, too.

We recommend that you describe the use of bottom-lining in coaching early in your work with coachees so they are not caught by surprise the first time you ask them to get to the bottom line. It's not that the particular story isn't interesting; in fact, it may be fascinating. But the story is the background, and in the coaching relationship, the background is secondary. With the limited time available for most coaching sessions, there simply isn't time for long-winded, detailed stories. You need to coach the essence, and asking coachees to get to the bottom line helps them discover the heart of the matter.

Bottom-lining is also an important skill for the coach. As the coach, you should not be talking much. Your conversation should be bottom-lined. Coachees do the talking.

Sample Dialogue

> **Coachee:** I know I'm starting to sound like a broken record on this, but there just wasn't time this week. Really, I'm not spinning a story here. I'm out of town one or two days a week . . . I'm still carrying the one evening class . . . I need to spend some time with my family . . .

> **COACH:** So what's the bottom line here, Tom?

> **Coachee:** I'm committed to helping my dad take care of Mom. God knows at his age—and with his own health issues—he could use the extra support. I just can't seem to live up to the time commitment to make it happen.

> **COACH:** What *will* you commit to—really commit to?

> **Coachee:** I don't control the travel—and being out of town just throws everything off . . . I don't see how . . .

> **COACH:** Bottom line, Tom. What will you commit to?

> **Coachee:** OK. One evening a week—somehow. And I can usually call him even when I'm out of town, so, more phone calls. I know he appreciates it . . .

Championing

We discussed acknowledgment earlier. Acknowledgment identifies an inner quality or shining attribute that you recognize in your coachee. When you describe it as an acknowledgment, coachees feel seen in important ways. To champion coachees is somewhat similar, but here the focus is on supporting coachees rather than identifying traits.

You champion coachees by standing up for them when they question their abilities or their capacity to take on the task of challenge. It is not empty cheerleading. As the coach, you champion what you know is true; coachees will know if you aren't sincere. When you're not sincere, you not only destroy the effect of the championing but you also put your own credibility at risk. But when you point out your coachees' abilities, their strengths, their resourcefulness and let them know you believe in them, you give them access to a little more of themselves.

Perhaps it is a capacity they didn't realize they had or strengths they don't give themselves credit for. You champion when the road is steep and the coachee is weary. That's when you recharge the coachee's enthusiasm: "You are so committed to this. I know you can do it." Or "You've shown over and over how you can be caring and firm. You can do it again." Or "You have the creative gifts—in abundance. You can do this." Championing is an affirmation. It is your capacity to see their capacity. It is a form of future looking. You see them at the finish line, the top of the hill, goals accomplished.

Sample Dialogue

Coachee: It's a great opportunity, a position I really want, but it's also a huge risk. Going for it, I could end up the world's biggest goat.

COACH: To mess with the Olympic slogan, I say, "Go for the goat!" I'm kidding. Let's go for the gold. What will it take to be the gold medal winner?

Coachee: To be absolutely honest, I don't think I see gold here—or silver or bronze for that matter. I'm not sure I belong in this race—now that I've seen some of the other candidates.

COACH: Now I'm not kidding. Mary, I know you can do this. It's a perfect match with your heart's desire and the path you laid out for yourself. You've got the skills to do it—and the panache to pull it off. Of course it's risky. That's where the adrenaline comes from, and that's why it feels like you're on the edge. I just know how you've worked to prepare for this. I know you can do this.

Coachee: I know you do. And it gives me confidence when I don't have much of my own.

Clearing

Clearing is that valuable skill of venting in order to become present and open to the coaching. A coachee could be in a thousand different emotional states or frames of mind as the coaching session begins. It could be that they've just been passed over for promotion; a friend has been in a serious traffic accident; their personal information has been hacked; they've been in a heated argument with a partner or coworker. Or, alternatively, they might start the session when they have just gotten back from vacation and their minds are still fogged with piña coladas or the euphoria of newfound love.

When coachees are preoccupied, it interferes with their ability to have useful, in-depth coaching conversations. Often, the need for clearing is obvious. The coachee is clearly disturbed, annoyed, upset, or agitated about something, and the something is big and present. However, the signs that tell the coach that clearing is called for may also be muted—you don't always hear huge alarms going off. The coachee may seem slightly miffed, or perhaps you sense a minor disturbance in the energy field. Initially, coachees may not even want to discuss it. But when you notice that their normal creative expression is blocked or constrained, you may need to push for clearing.

Imagine that your coachee is clearly annoyed about some injustice. There's a mood about her that hangs in the air like an unpleasant odor. You might say, "You seem really blocked. Let's take a couple of minutes to get this out. Really complain, whine, feel sorry for yourself. Exaggerate." The best thing you can do at this point is to help the coachee clear. In fact, it is important that the coach recognize the volume of clearing necessary.

Coachees often feel awkward about just venting and want to quit before they're completely clear. So you must really push until the last gasp of bad air is out. Make it a game and keep pressing for more: "Turn up the volume. What else happened? And then what? How did that feel? What a jerk! Tell me more."

Sample Dialogue

> **COACH:** You seem distracted—it's like we're having to work too hard to stay on track this morning.
>
> **Coachee:** I am distracted. I lost $2,500 yesterday in a stupid stock deal. I feel like an idiot.
>
> **COACH:** It sounds like you need to clear that before we can move on.
>
> **Coachee:** I think you're right.
>
> **COACH:** Take a minute. Ventilate.
>
> **Coachee:** I feel like a chump. Worse than that, I convinced two of my friends that this was the sweetest deal in a century, and they both lost money, too.

COACH: Ouch. What else? Let's turn up the volume.

Coachee: Okay. I'm mad at myself for getting sucked into an "easy money" scheme. I'm ashamed about looking like an easy mark.

COACH: Go for it. What else?

Coachee: I'm afraid my wife's going to shoot me. I let her and the kids down. How am I going to come up with another $2,500 for vacation this summer?

COACH: You feel like you let your family down. . . . What else?

Coachee: I should have seen this one coming.

COACH: So you've got a judgment—"should have seen this coming." What else?

Coachee: It's a pretty empty feeling.

COACH: There you are in emptiness. What's next?

Coachee: I think I need to get past the sour feeling.

COACH: How will you do that?

Coachee: This clearing is a good start. I think I'll plan on taking a long walk with my wife. The sooner we deal with this, the better, and we do love a long walk.

COACH: Is there more? Is this the issue you want to be working on today?

Coachee: No, actually, thanks for asking. I'll do the walk tonight if I can. In the meantime, I've got something more pressing for today.

Reframing

Coachees frequently get stuck with a certain way of looking at a situation or an experience. Their perspective, moreover, has a message that is in some way disabling. Your ability to reframe the experience provides a fresh perspective and a sense of renewed possibility. Imagine this scenario: Your coachee had his hopes set on landing a major consulting contract and just found out it has been put on hold for at least six months. Naturally, he is focused on the disappointment. As his coach, you point out that it gives him the time he has been seeking to write a series of articles that can help him land new business. Thus you are able to recast this experience in terms of his ultimate goals. Using much the same data, you interpret the experience in a way that includes more of the coachee's life: the big picture.

In fact, reframing works just as effectively if you ask your coachee to do the reframing. In the previous example, it might sound like this: "I hear your disappointment. How could you use the six months to lay the groundwork for other new business?"

Reframing requires looking on the bright side of things, true enough, but it involves more than just being perky for the coachee. Reframing offers more than clichéd comfort—as in "There are plenty of fish in the sea" or "Tomorrow's another day." Reframing takes real pieces of the coachee's life and shifts the perspective to show an opportunity or a pathway that wasn't apparent minutes before.

Imagine that your coachee is struggling with credit card debt and tells you that it's hard to make progress, especially when major appliances break down and need repair. You point out that she has managed to change her buying habits and has regularly paid down her outstanding balance for several months. The reframing doesn't change the fact that it is a struggle. But it does show the coachee that she is resourceful and committed—and making progress. Reframing changes the theme from "Credit cards have control of my life" to "I have control of my life."

Sample Dialogue

In this case, the coachee starts with a certain perspective: He has wasted six weeks developing a business plan that reached a dead end. Still, he learned a lot that will help with new business plans, and he made several good contacts. In short, there is plenty that is positive in this experience. And that's where the coach is headed: to reinforce the action and learning that accompanied this effort.

> **Coachee:** Absolutely a dead end. Now nothing. Six weeks shot to hell.
>
> **COACH:** You followed a path that looked very promising six weeks ago. I remember you were pretty excited.
>
> **Coachee:** I was excited.
>
> **COACH:** What did you learn in those six weeks?

Coachee: I learned how to write a business plan. Not that it did me much good.

COACH: What else did you learn?

Coachee: I learned how to present my business to people outside my field.

COACH: Nontechnical people?

Coachee: Yeah. Bankers and venture capitalists.

COACH: What else did you learn?

Coachee: I guess I learned that this is something I can do—even though I don't enjoy it as much as I enjoy the engineering.

COACH: In that case, what's your assessment of the last six weeks?

Coachee: I wish I could have had the same learning in half the time. And now that I've got the presentation formatted, and practiced, I might as well keep giving it to investors until somebody sees the opportunity and backs my plan.

COACH: Great. What do you want to do about that this week?

Making Distinctions

Reframing is one way of helping coachees see a situation from a fresh perspective. Another way is to help them pull apart collapsed beliefs by making clear distinctions where two or more have been tangled into one limiting, often disempowering, belief. The belief appears to be a fact of life, and it's not. It can sound like, "Well—as everyone knows . . . "

For example, let's say a coachee believes that because she's the manager in charge of the department and its results, she needs to be the expert: the reliable authority who has all the answers. She has a constant fear that someone on her team will ask a question she can't immediately answer and that her credibility and authority will vanish in humiliation. The separate facts are that she is the manager and that there are team members with expertise and experience she doesn't have. As her coach, you have the objectivity to see the distinction. You might say something like, "It sounds like you have these two things locked up as one: you are the manager—therefore you have to have all the answers. What if that isn't true?"

Sample Dialogues

Coach Practitioner

Coachee: I plan every week. I use a planner. I take the time on Sunday night to plan my week. None of it helps. By Tuesday, my week is in shambles.

COACH: What happens when you try to stick to your plan?

Coachee: People make requests. They've got urgent things they need from me—things I didn't necessarily have in my plan—so wham, it's all out of kilter.

COACH: What happens if you say no?

Coachee: Not in this organization. It doesn't work that way. If you're going to succeed around here, you have to move fast, be flexible, respond to the fire that's burning. That's what they mean by "teamwork" in this company.

COACH: Sounds like you end up paying a pretty high price for that. It also sounds like you've got a couple of things tangled together. What if we try to separate them?

Coachee: Like what? I'm not following you.

COACH: You seem to be saying, "When people make requests of me, I need to abandon my plan."

Coachee: I'd say that's true in this organization.

COACH: So . . . would you be willing to play along with me here? I'd like to find an alternative point of view, just to give you some additional perspective.

Coachee: Sure.

COACH: Here are the two facts: people make requests, and you have a plan. In the past, you've said yes to the requests automatically. What would be another way to deal with requests?

Coachee: I could postpone saying yes by telling people I have to check my calendar first.

COACH: Good. What would be another way?

Coachee: I suppose I could learn to say no sometimes.

Manager and Direct Report

Direct Report: Hey, Mary Ellen, do you have a few minutes?

Manager: I do, actually. What's up?

Direct Report: I have a situation with some of the team members, and I can't seem to work it out. I need some guidance. It's not getting better.

Manager: How can I help?

Direct Report: I want to be fair to everyone on the team. I'm basically the one who hands out projects. Some are exciting and creative . . . some are, frankly, dull. You know. You were in this role once.

Manager: I do know. And it sounds like there is a disturbance in the fairness factor.

Direct Report: We have some genuine high achievers on the team—you've seen their work. They're grumbling, not always to me. They think they should get more of the pearls and fewer of the stones.

Manager: And I heard you say that you want to be fair to everyone on the team.

Direct Report: I do. I think it's important that everyone shares equally—in the exciting and the more mundane.

Manager: As team leader, what's the crux of the issue for you?

Direct Report: How do I keep the high achievers happy and still create a sense of fairness?

Manager: Can I share an observation?

Direct Report: I'm all ears.

Manager: It sounds like you had two things collapsed together. As you've described it, "fairness" equaled "everyone does the same work." Now you've pulled those two ideas apart. So the new question is this: *What does fairness look like on a team where there are genuinely high performers?*

Direct Report: You're not going to give me the answer to that, are you?

Manager: No. That's the team leader's job.

These are classic examples of collapsed beliefs that can be separated so that coachees can escape from traps they have created for themselves. In the process of pulling them apart, all sorts of new possibilities emerge.

Exercises

1. Self-Management

Where are you likely to get hooked in the midst of a coaching conversation? Where are you most likely to need self-management? List 10 things your coachee might say that would pull you to Level I. For example: "I don't think you're listening to me." Next, list 10 things you can do to return to the coaching conversation and stay engaged.

Get to know your coaching self-judgments. Where do you automatically find fault with your coaching? You could make a list or spend some time in self-reflection. The more aware you are of these judgments, the less likely you are to be hooked by them in the middle of a coaching session.

What are the topics you tend to avoid? Which topics make you feel inadequate, inexperienced, or simply uncomfortable? For managers, where do you get trapped into instantly wanting to fix things? What are the situations where you get hooked?

2. Championing

Pull out that list of 10 friends or colleagues from chapter 3 one more time. Call, write, or email them as their champion. Here's the key. Yes, you believe they can do "it"—whatever the "it" is for them. The question for you as coach is this: How do you know? That's where the essence of championing lives. There is reason, there is evidence—you know they can because_____ . Fill in that blank. Then let them know they can do the things they need to do. Without the clear sense of how you know, championing sounds like mere flattery, empty. When you ground it in what you already know, the belief in them can stand tall.

3. Clearing

Train a friend or a colleague in the skill of clearing so that he or she can clear you. Your partner's job is to encourage you to go deeper, to turn up the volume until you reach the bottom of whatever it is you are trying to clear. This person doesn't need to understand what's going on with you; the point is to prompt you to vent, like cheering an athlete to the finish line.

Then select an area of your life where you need clearing and process the clearing exercise with your partner. When it is over, talk with that person or make notes about what happened as you became clear. What happened to the "charge" when you allowed yourself to express it completely?

Co-Active Principles

In part 3 we will look at the three core principles in the co-active model—fulfillment, balance, and process. They represent three aspects of a life fully lived. These three entry points in the coaching relationship connect to a deeper quality of life and offer three lenses through which coachee and coach can see—even magnify—the impact of the choices coachees make that create their life experience.

In coaching, the presenting issue for the conversation can take an unlimited number of forms. It might be a goal to achieve, a decision to make, a new practice to acquire, a habit to break, or an issue to resolve. It is the visible outcome and the main focus of the conversation between coach and coachee whether they have a formal, professional relationship or they are the manager and a direct report. In the co-active approach, this conversation is a collaboration, and the five contexts are what the coach brings in order to create the optimal conditions for the coachee's outcome.

The presenting issue is the reason for the coaching interaction. However, there is an even deeper purpose at the most compelling heart of co-active coaching. It may not always be visible or placed in the spotlight of the moment, but it is there, uniquely defined by every individual, a resonant expression of these three principles: fulfillment, balance, and process.

Every choice that coachees make leads somewhere. The choices are not in isolation; they reverberate in the coachee's life, sometimes (but not always) profoundly. Even when those choices seem ordinary, as uninspiring but necessary actions, they are nonetheless connected to the coachee's quality of life. Those everyday choices have the power over time to create a more fulfilling life, an approach that balances life's many choices, and a process that leads to a life fully lived, fully expressed, fully experienced.

In this section of the book, we describe each core principle, describe the practices associated with coaching those principles, and provide exercises and examples for coaches where applicable.

CHAPTER 8

Fulfillment

Think about your own life for a moment. What is your vision of a really fulfilling life? What would that be like? Savor that thought. Notice that the question—with the word *fulfilling* in it—takes you deeper than simply asking, "What do you want?" This greater depth is the reason that fulfillment is one of the three core principles in co-active coaching.

Let's be honest. Most people don't come to coaching saying, "What I want is a more fulfilling life"—at least not in those exact words. It's not likely foremost in the mind of your direct reports when they knock on your office door asking if you have a few minutes. In either case, they typically have something much more specific and urgent on their mind. In the moment, they may not have any awareness that there is a connection between this specific situation and a more fulfilling life or work life experience. But the connection is there underneath—an ever-present yearning for something even deeper. A fulfilling life is a life of meaning, purpose, satisfaction.

We believe that this yearning is like the keel of a boat in the lives of your coachees; it is the shape of their lives beneath the surface that keeps them on course. Without that keel, a boat will drift and shift directions on the vagaries of the wind. One of the most valuable things we do for coachees is to help them get clear about that very personal shape of fulfillment and how it connects to this momentary question arising on the surface. The tools of fulfillment coaching help coachees find that connection.

It sounds simple enough. But in our experience, it takes tremendous courage and commitment on the part of the coachee to really choose and keep choosing a course of fulfillment. The world we live in is designed to squeeze people into boxes—often very comfortable boxes, but boxes nonetheless. Pressures at work are designed to get short-term results: to make things happen. Consequently, there's little time for exploration as expansive as "how this contributes to my fulfilling life."

Choosing to create a truly fulfilling life is almost certain to upset the status quo and create ripples in the pond. That's the nature of setting fulfilling goals and getting into action. And yet when the connection is present, when this action to be taken is a fractal of fulfillment, the everyday moment is transformative. It's important for coaches to understand the scale and impact of fulfillment as they begin their work with coachees.

The Hunger for Fulfillment

Part of the difficulty in creating a fulfilling life starts with where coachees have their attention. As they look for ways to have a more fulfilling life, they look at what they have . . . and what they don't have . . . and see a gap. Then they look for things to fill the gap—something that will make their lives more fulfilling. That "something" can be the obvious: a higher-paying job, a vacation home, a successful business. The search can also focus on getting things that are less tangible: a wonderful marriage or a promotion.

Unfortunately, having things is momentary, and the satisfaction is fleeting. You know that from your own life. Think of something you really wanted to have. Think about the moment of delight when you acquired it and how quickly the glow began to fade: six months after the new car, or the new promotion, or the new relationship. A "fulfilling life" is not something you attain by accomplishment or acquisition. It is a continuous process of creation. As long as we continue to look for *things* to define our fulfillment, we are likely to be temporarily filled and constantly hungry.

To Be Fulfilled

Co-active coaching creates a different frame for fulfillment. It asks coachees to look at what it would take to be fulfilled. And not just "some day in the future" when the goal is reached, but today, because fulfillment is available every day of our lives. That is the stand we take in the co-active approach. Of course, envisioning a future that is even more fulfilling is by itself a fulfilling exercise. Working toward goals that make the vision real is also fulfilling right now, in this moment, because we are consciously moving toward a more fulfilled life. The point is that fulfillment is an exercise of choice and not something that will happen "as soon as I _____ " (fill in the blank).

Part of the confusion about fulfillment is in the language. We know what it means to be "full," so we think fulfillment is a state we will eventually reach: filled, capped off, finished. Instead, fulfillment is a paradox in that we can be filled today and filled again tomorrow, maybe even in a different way, and then be filled again the next day and the day after that. It is disillusioning to try to capture fulfillment. "Having" fulfillment is like trying to bottle daylight.

This doesn't mean that your coachees will stop wanting to have things in their lives. Coachees will still want to have things: a successful business, more money, romantic relationships. But these things are the expressions of their fulfillment. They are not fulfillment itself.

Feeling Good Is Not a Sign

This is an important distinction. We often confuse being fulfilled with feeling good. The two conditions may coexist, but that is not necessary. In a state of fulfillment, there's often a sense of effortlessness—of harmony and congruence with the great laws of the universe. But fulfillment can also exist when life is difficult, challenging, or uncomfortable. Some people will say that the times when they felt most fulfilled were times when they had the least, when life was a struggle. They were doing what was important to them—things that claimed their passion and commitment. Ask team members about the most fulfilling experiences in their career life and they are very likely to recount tales of overcoming enormous challenges; these were not easy times, but they were deeply rewarding.

There, in the midst of scarcity or struggle, life was abundant and energized. Perhaps the simplicity of the time or the sharp focus gave them a clearer picture of what was truly valuable and fulfilling for them, but their sense of fulfillment was not about feeling good or being happy all the time. Living a life of purpose, mission, or service can be intense, sometimes heartbreaking and exhausting, and at the same time enormously fulfilling. The paradox of fulfillment is that it is possible both to have a sense of inner peace and to experience an outer struggle at the same time.

To Be Alive

In fact, describing fulfillment may be as simple as this: Fulfillment is about being fully alive. Fulfillment is the state of fully expressing who we are and doing what is right for us. Coachees have a sense of that feeling. They describe it as wholeness, satisfaction, a sense of rightness and harmony.

A word we use for this feeling is *resonance*. Life is vibrating at a frequency at which everything we most value is in alignment. We feel it in the choices we make. The vibration in the moment may be very dramatic, thunderous, exciting, edgy. Or it may be still, serene, pastel, intimate. It might be a unique combination of all of those qualities—defying physics and our metaphors. But coachees will feel the resonance. The pieces of their lives or careers come together in a very personal sense of wholeness and of feeling very alive. It may be experienced through doing meaningful work, feeling well used, contributing, giving and receiving, playing to win, being in the flow, expressing their creativity. It is an experience of being complete.

That resonant feeling, when action and deep purpose are aligned, is an enormous engine for motivation as well. Making the connection fuels the desire and commitment and will help coachees when the hill is steep or the headwinds strong.

Big Agenda—Little Agenda

In co-active coaching, we see an agenda that is always on the table even if it is not always articulated. This is the big agenda, and it is at the heart of the coaching: it is the coachee's full, resonant life. This is a life that is lived from the coachee's values. It is in dynamic action, balancing the coachee's priorities in life, and it is lived fully in each moment. Coachees are completely in the process of living. There is an underlying question that coach and coachee are always tuned to, even if it is not always surfaced: *What do you want your life to be?* In this question, the emphasis is on the *being* state. In fulfillment coaching, we look for the coachee's big agenda with questions such as *What is your vision? Who are you becoming? What is present when life is most alive for you?*

There is also an ongoing conversation about action and the doing of life; otherwise, coaching would be nothing more than very interesting contemplative conversation. Action is where coachees make that fulfilling life real; it's the "active" part of co-active. This is the little agenda. It is not little by comparison or less important, and it is certainly not to be minimized. Rather, it is simply a convenient way to talk about both aspects of fulfillment. Both are essential. The little agenda consists of goals, action, and accountability. With each coaching session, there is an issue to work on, plans to make, goals to define, and accountability to create action and learning.

In this model, the little agenda leads to fulfilling the big agenda. That is crucial. Part of the coach's job is to hold this meta-view for coachees, probing to make sure that the action being contemplated is aligned with the coachee's resonant, fully alive life—and not motivated by circumstances, fear, or a corrupted sense of duty.

Fulfillment and Values

Imagine you could do what brings you the greatest joy or deepest satisfaction: be with the people you love, use your natural talents, exploit your gifts to their fullest. That would indeed be fulfilling. It is a picture of a person living according to what he or she values most.

The link between values and fulfillment is so obvious that it may be overlooked. Helping coachees discover and clarify their values is a way to create a map that will guide them along the decision paths of their lives. When you clarify values with your coachees, you learn more about what makes them tick: what's important and what's not. Coachees discover what is truly essential to them in their lives. This helps them take a stand and make choices based on what is fulfilling to them.

Honoring our values is inherently fulfilling even when it is hard. If authenticity is a very high value for your coachees, they may find there are times when they must suffer discomfort in order to live according to that value. The discomfort will pass, and a sense of integrity or congruency with their values will remain. When that value is not honored, however, the coachee feels internal tension or dissonance. Because human beings are flexible and resilient, it is possible to absorb a tremendous amount of discord and keep going, but there is a very high price to pay—a sense of selling out on oneself—and the result is a life of toleration or betrayal rather than fulfillment.

Values, Not Morals or Principles

Values are not morals. There is no sense of morally right or wrong behavior here. Values are not about moral character or ethical behavior, though living in a highly ethical way may be a value. Values are not principles either, like self-government or standards of behavior. Values are the qualities of a life lived fully from the inside out. There is nothing inherently virtuous in your coachee's values. What is to be admired is not the value itself but your coachee's ability to live that value fully in his or her life. When we honor our values and the choices we make in our lives, we feel an internal "rightness." It's as if each value produces its own special tone. When we live our values, the various tones create a unique harmony. When we are not living our values, there is dissonance. The discord can get so extreme, so jarring, that it can become physically unhealthy.

What is important for leaders and managers to know is that values show up in choices and those choices are visible in behavior. You are modeling your values in every moment and so are the people who report to you. As a leader, your action—the decisions you make or don't make, how you treat people, everything—is done under the sharp eye of those who report to you or who are under your leadership. They are watching you. By your action you set the tone and, in fact, reveal constantly what you value. Having a list of corporate values posted in prominent places is a fine idea. How you act and react will be more powerful in reinforcing behavior than that list. Actions truly do speak louder than words.

Employees' values show up in their behavior, too. By looking for the values in their behavior, you can learn what's important to them, what they prioritize, how they make choices, and how those choices impact working relationships. Without ever doing a formal "values clarification" exercise, you can see what matters to them. For example, you may have one employee who places a very high value on respect and inclusion. Another member of the team may place a very high value on getting things done and driving for results. Both team members make choices based on those values, and in their collaboration they sometimes find themselves in an impasse because of a clash of those two value propositions. There is no right or wrong here. It is an example of how looking beyond the visible conflict can help reveal values.

Values Clarification

Values are intangible. They are not something we do or have. Money, for example, is not a value, although money as a resource could lead to honoring values such as fun, creativity, achievement, peace of mind, and service to others. Travel is not a value. Gardening is not a value. But both are examples of cherished activities that honor certain values, including adventure, learning, nature, and spirituality. And yet, although values are intangible, they are not invisible to others. You can walk into a room of strangers and get a sense of what people value by what they wear, how they stand in the room, how and with whom they interact, and the topics of their conversations. You can sense the values in the room: power, friendship, intimacy, connection, independence, fun, and more.

As coach, you will be able to help coachees clarify their values as you hear about their lives, their action, the things they choose and don't choose. You will see them when they honor their values and when they don't, and you will both learn something either way. This is one of the reasons why you will return to the values clarification process from time to time.

Because our language is imprecise, it's often easier to cluster values than to try to invest all the meaning in a single word. Thus, we might separate a series of value attributes with slash marks to indicate a grouping of value words that communicates a composite sense. For example, *freedom/risk taking/adventure* is different from *freedom/independence/choice*.

In practice, the words are not as important as the coachee's ability to feel the impact of that value. All of these values or value clusters will be unique to each person. Just as our physical features give us our unique appearance, the articulation, prioritization, and clarity of our values determine our individual identity. It's not even important that you, as coach, understand exactly what coachees mean by the words they choose. It is enough that coachees are clear about what the words represent, so when they find they're off track, the wording of their values can help set them back on course. In fact, the coachee's own unique metaphor or expression very often is better than the common vocabulary at capturing the sense of the value. Coachees may have values like these:

- Coyote/wild dancer/mischief maker
- Luminous/chenille/lavender
- Standing ovation/going for it/buzzer beater

The unique, personal expression conveys more energy than a word from the dictionary and ultimately creates more commitment to have more of that value in their life.

The Value of Values Clarification

The most effective way to clarify values is to extract them from the coachee's life experience. Ask coachees to describe the values they see in their own lives, perhaps clustered together, using their own words. Almost any life situation can be used to mine for values, but those that have a strong impact, either positive or negative, are especially productive. This way, values rise naturally out of the coachee's life instead of being selected off a checklist. When coachees are presented with a list, they are often tempted to go shopping for values: "This would be nice to have . . . people would admire this." Because people tend to judge their values, they often list values they think they should have, like spirituality or integrity, and exclude the ones that society says are not so admirable, such as personal power and recognition.

Values are either present in or absent from the choices coachees make every day, which means that any given daily activity can be linked to a value honored or a value betrayed. As coach, you might ask: "Where is this value showing up?" "What values do you sometimes neglect?" "Which are the values you will not compromise?" Once you have worked with a coachee to develop a personal list of values, another fruitful exercise is to ask the coachee to prioritize the values, ranking the top 10 from the most important on down.

The outcome of the exercise, a prioritized list, is not as important as the process itself. Clearly, the coachee is free to change the order of items on that list anytime. The prioritizing exercise forces coachees to feel the unique qualities of each value and, by sorting the values in a particular order, to feel the special importance of each one. Some coaches set the stage by making it a kind of game: "If you can take only five values with you into a strange and possibly dangerous territory, which are the ones you absolutely must have?" By amplifying the stakes, coaches ensure that coachees raise their own awareness about the values that most matter in their lives.

The next step is to ask coachees how they are honoring these values on a scale of 1 to 10, with 1 meaning the value is not at all present in their lives, and 10 meaning it is honored completely all the time. There are almost certain to be values that are ranked at 4, 5, or 6 in some important aspect of the coachee's life—most likely a place where there is upset, anger, or resentment because the important value is getting neglected or in some cases, betrayed. It's a great opportunity for coaching: "What's that about?" "What would it take to live that value in those circumstances?" "What is the price you pay for not honoring that value?" "What's stopping you?"

As manager, you may not go through an exercise of values clarification with each member of your team. You could, and there would be great benefit for that. It would give you great insight into where that employee is likely to be focused, the strongest forces that impact decisions, even where there are possible blind spots. But simply tuning your attention to the impact of values as they show up in behavior will give you added insight into how employees make decisions, how they communicate with others, how they manage resources, or how they approach new and challenging assignments. As manager you can begin to see the intent and motivation behind the behavior.

Coaching Fulfillment

As you can see, fulfillment is intensely personal; it is also constantly evolving. What was fulfilling at age twenty-five may have lost its fascination by thirty-five; the empire-building passion of thirty-five may give way to a search for inner peace by forty-five. It is important to help the coachee develop a clear picture of a fulfilling life as it is today. To that end, there are a number of practical ways to help people clarify their personal definitions of fulfillment, and you can continue to use these tools in an ongoing relationship to refine that vision. (For more information about specific tools, see the Co-Active Online Toolkit: *coactive.com/toolkit.*)

Level of Satisfaction

For a big-picture snapshot of where the coachee is in terms of fulfillment on any given day, the Wheel of Life (see figure 5) is a very effective device. As you and the coachee look at each area in the wheel, discuss the state of the coachee's fulfillment on a scale of 1 to 10. Ask how fulfilled he or she is in the area of money, or relationships, or health and wellness, for example. Or what a fulfilled life would be like in the area of career.

Notice that you are not asking what the coachee needs to have in order to be fulfilled in his or her career. The question is *What would it take to be fulfilled?* Then keep probing in that direction. Whatever comes up, follow it with *What else?* or *Tell me more.* The idea is to uncover deeper and deeper levels of meaning and, from time to time, to clarify what you hear and play it back to your coachees so they can hear what they're saying. For example, you might approach it like this: "I heard you say you'd like a sense of security when it comes to money—a sense that there will

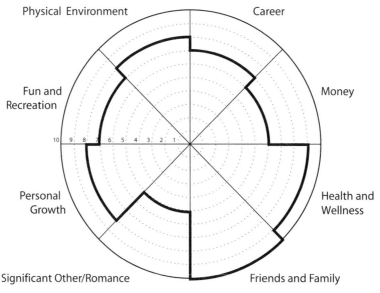

FIGURE 5   Wheel of Life: Fulfillment

be enough in an emergency. It sounds like security might be a value. Is that right?"

Using the Wheel of Life, coachees will see for themselves the parts of their lives where they are unfulfilled. With your help, coachees will go through a process that allows them to define what fulfillment means to them. For example, you might begin, "In health and wellness, you say your sense of fulfillment is 6. What would it take to raise that 6 to 10? What will you do to make it fulfilling?"

For managers, a variation on this exercise is to have the employee design a "Wheel of Life at Work," with each of the areas a significant part of that person's work and career. Ask questions like *What would a fulfilling life at work include? What is your current score for each of those areas?*

Values and Decision Making

In coaching, values help determine the "rightness" of choices. They also illuminate unfortunate choices. Coachees can look back over decisions they've made and see where their values were honored or were ignored. For you as coach, knowing the coachee's values is a tremendous advantage. You can quickly see how certain courses of action will be blessed with a sense of flow and ease because the activities are congruent with the coachee's values. By knowing when the coachee's values are not being honored, you can also see the potential iceberg in front of the *Titanic*.

A values conversation can be very useful at any decision point. As coachees choose various action steps, their values become a litmus test for action: *Will this action move you closer to living your values or further away? If you make this decision, what values will be present?* When the coachee is considering an important life decision, ask how this course of action will honor the top 10 values and to what extent. A decision based on the coachee's top values will always be a more fulfilling decision. It may not be the easiest or the most enjoyable. It may require sacrifice and even have uncomfortable consequences. But on balance, over time, it will be the most fulfilling.

We have seen the opposite too often. Again and again, coachees have made decisions based on their bank balance, or their fear of creating discomfort, or their worry about others' displeasure. They decide based on what is easiest at the moment or will make the fewest waves. Such decisions never work out for the coachees' fulfillment because they have sold out on themselves and their values. (See the Co-Active Online Toolkit for more on values clarification. *coactive.com/toolkit*)

Fulfillment and Life Purpose

A life purpose statement is another way of capturing the essence of what it means to be fully alive—living life intentionally, making choices that increase the value of life to one's self and to others. Like standing on the top of a tall hill, coachees see their life in a larger context. They ask, *What is my unique contribution to my family, my work, my community? What difference do I make with my life?* Living a life that includes following a purpose-directed path—that's deeply fulfilling. In this way, fulfillment reaches out into the world and yet loops back to enrich that one life.

Having a sense of purpose has become a key element in job searching and job satisfaction as well. People are looking for more than a job with a paycheck; they are looking for meaningful work where, at the end of the day, they can feel they contributed, they made a difference. Finding purpose at work can be enormously motivating and deeply engaging.

There are many ways to elicit the coachee's life purpose, and there is more than one way to describe this definition of what our lives are about. Some call it a "mission statement" or a "vision statement." It gets to the heart of what a person's true life legacy will be—the difference this life will make.

The life purpose is a path, not a destination. And along the way, coachees will encounter plenty of voices, internal and external, telling them to go in other directions. Sometimes they will listen, especially when they are unsure of their purpose. Finding and claiming a life purpose gives coachees a powerful sense of direction for their lives. The truth they find in the life purpose statement can make them virtually unstoppable.

Defining one's life purpose is a process that usually takes time. It can involve personal reflection, reading, keeping a journal, or interviewing others. Finding the one statement that rings true requires peeling back the layers until the coachee reaches the statement that addresses the central questions of his or her life: *What is the hunger I am here to feed? Where is the pain I can ease? What is the teaching I am called to do? Where is the building I have the tools to accomplish?*

Life purpose is about coachees using their talents as well as the unique learning of their lives, their experience, and their wisdom. A fulfilled life is one they are able to live with purpose—intentionally, not by accident. (A number of exercises in the Co-Active Online Toolkit are designed to help coachees clarify a life purpose statement. *coactive.com/toolkit*)

The life purpose statement has value in coaching because it focuses attention on a fully alive, fully expressed, fulfilling life. The coaching that goes into creating the life purpose statement is rich with self-discovery, values clarification, and vision. Coachees are challenged to use all the talents they have been given. It is also a fruitful place for acknowledgment when coachees make the sometimes difficult decision to follow their purpose instead of taking the easier way. Living a life of meaning and purpose is a rare accomplishment indeed, and in one sense it is the very definition of fulfillment.

Dissonance

When you are honoring your values regularly and consistently, you might say you have a formula for living happily ever after. In that case, why don't we honor our values all the time? There are a hundred variations on the answer to that very good question. A common theme is that our fear is stronger than our desire for fulfillment. That fear, which leads to self-sabotage, comes in a variety of guises.

If a coachee is not making choices based on his or her values, then the effect will be some form of dissonance. It can be frustration, boredom, indifference, anger, resignation, or persistent justification for a course of action that looks very much like self-betrayal or martyrdom. As a coach, you will be able to sense it in the air. It may have the acrid smell of fear, or it may be masked in the fragrance of flowery rationalizations. As you use your Level III awareness to listen between the words, you will feel the dissonance. It may be a disturbance in the force—something is not quite right.

Coachees may believe that this voice is trying to protect them from danger, loss of relationship, a catastrophe of some kind. The voice is there to keep coachees from taking unsafe risks, but it is often overcautious at a time that calls for risks for the sake of change and a more fulfilling life. This dissonant voice is the voice of an internal saboteur. The same voice may recite an old litany of judgment, rules, and limiting beliefs. It says things like "You aren't working hard enough." "You should be further along in your career." "You don't do well on tests." Basically, the message is that you're not smart enough, attractive enough, wealthy enough, experienced enough, old enough . . . you're not enough. Or it could be the opposite: you're too old, bald, frumpy, young, aggressive, introverted, extroverted . . . you're too much.

Most of the time, this voice operates quietly in the background, influencing choices and lobbying for its preferred course of action or inaction. Be aware that whenever people take the initiative to change their lives, an alarm sounds and the saboteur will awaken. Expect it. You can even forewarn your coachees.

Fulfillment and the Coach's Role

Fulfillment sounds so good—like a really great meal—satisfying, tasty, and ultimately filling. And yet the path to fulfillment can be difficult, unfamiliar, and scary for coachees. Choosing to live our lives based on our values is not what society has taught us to do. It is not the easy, well-trodden way. Most of us settle for what we can have. We make choices based on what others want, what would be easiest, what would cause the least discomfort. We tolerate. We compromise. We give up. It's no easy task to get on the track for fulfillment or to stay on track after that path has been chosen. This is why we emphasize that choosing a fulfilling life is a radical act.

The coach's role is to challenge coachees to pursue their fulfillment, in spite of the circumstances, in spite of the voices all around them offering bad advice and contrary agendas, and in spite of the coachee's own inner saboteur. When the road forward looks hard and dark, and the light of the power of fulfilling choices is dim, your job as coach is to be out front, encouraging, pointing the way to a life fully lived, a life that is valued and without regret.

Remember that this big agenda is, at the core, the most life-giving choice coachees can make. Whatever results coachees achieve on their goals and plans, this is the true satisfaction for them and the coaches who serve them: that at the end of the day, there is more life in each day.

CHAPTER 9

Balance

In the co-active model, balance is one of the three core principles because it is fundamental to the quality of life. At least, if you ask coachees, that's what they say. Over and over again, coachees tell us that they want more balance in their lives. This issue of balance exists on two levels: the underlying quality of life and the day-to-day experience.

In the big picture, fulfillment is about living a life that is valued, purposeful, and alive, and balance is about choosing a life that is in action, aligned with a compelling vision. When it comes to balance, what coachees want is the ability to juggle the precious priorities of their lives. They want more tools to manage their activities and relationships so that these relationships and activities line up and move forward. Coachees want to be more empowered and less at the mercy of circumstances and other people's expectations and demands. They want to feel they are choosing their life, not just reacting to it.

They don't necessarily want all the pieces of their lives to have the same weight. Balance is not about evening out everything. Balance also should not be confused with reaching some ultimate equilibrium. There is no static point in life; life is inherently dynamic. We are constantly balancing.

Balance is not about slowing down, although slowing down may be just the recipe some days. Balance is not about simplifying, although sorting out the pieces, choosing "yes" to some things and "no" to others, may be the ideal way to create the most fulfilling flow. In short, what most coachees want is not to go faster or slower or to have less or more, but to have a life-giving ride supported on the rails of a fulfilling life vision. How they get that ride is the objective of balance coaching. Note that some coachees want a smoother ride and some want the exhilaration of a bumpy ride, at least from time to time, and balance coaching can help them make that choice, too.

Inside the organization, the pressure is on to be in action in multiple directions for multiple priorities, deadlines, and commitments—all at the same time. A balance-oriented conversation won't change the driving pace of expectations, but it will help people make choices from a place of flow and alignment, rather than simply reacting out of urgency. For managers, the tools of balance help team members choose more effectively; they help employees perform more consistently with more flow and hit the guardrails less frequently.

Day to Day

That said, coachees are not likely to come to coaching with "a more balanced life" at the top of their list. That's not where their attention is. They're focused on the issues that are hitting them on the chin that day or that week: the pressing deadline, the career-accelerating opportunity, the dreaded family reunion, the credit card debt, the new relationship. They have their attention on the action of their lives, especially in those areas where they are not getting the results they want. After all, that's why they are working with a coach—so they can get the desired results.

Coachees may see themselves as blocked, at a crossroads or a dead end, even out of options. They may feel resigned, defeated, or simply frustrated and confused. They may feel powerless, lost, or trapped in a repeating cycle. In your eagerness to help coachees move forward, you, as coach, may be tempted to break the problems down into bite-sized bits and brainstorm solutions, to get results quickly and move past all that sluggishness or spinning wildly. Instead, balance coaching starts with the way coachees look at the situation; the need for different action is not the starting point. The coachee's point of view is often the main contributing factor to the blocked, stuck, or spinning feeling.

Balance coaching is designed to restore flow, to get coachees into action on today's issues in a way that brings them back into alignment and back in control of their own lives. Balance coaching begins by looking at the boxes in which coachees find themselves, because the limitations of those boxes are impeding their progress. In doing so, coachees restore flow to those immediate areas and, in the process, learn important lessons about creating more flow in their lives. They learn to be more adept at seeing the boxes that hold them in, and the patterns of their own obstruction. What they learn by breaking out of those boxes serves them in other areas. This is how balance coaching works with the big agenda.

As a leadership competency, balance is about the choices leaders make for their personal sense of creating flow, but it is also about the impact of their leadership. The choices leaders make lead to more balance or less for the team and organization, and in the process they become the visible creators and models for how choices are made in that culture. The degree to which there is consistent flow is a direct reflection of their leadership.

Circumstances versus Possibilities

There are always reasons why coachees are not getting the results they want. Just listen and they will tell you. The reasons almost always sound realistic and convincing. When you begin listening underneath those explanations, you will hear a particular tone or flavor that accompanies the reasons and rationalizations. You will hear about difficult situations and uncontrollable circumstances. You will hear about rigid timelines and expectations, people who are inflexible or unwilling. It may or may not sound like complaining, and it might sound quite normal and perfectly understandable.

This can be a particular trap for leaders and managers because they live and work immersed in the same circumstances as the team members and employees. It can be easy to hear a direct report describe the impeding struggles and complications and find yourself nodding in agreement. The truth is, there are things that coachees—or leaders for that matter—simply do not have control over. That's not a perspective. It's real. But the conversation doesn't need to stop there. The question then becomes, "What *do* you have control over? What choices *are* possible?"

In fulfillment, you tune your ear to hear the aliveness of values being lived, honored, and celebrated—a sense of purpose, a future envisioned. Or you could hear the opposite: deadness, anger, crankiness. In balance, you will hear a life in flow filled with possibilities and alternative courses of action, freedom, and creativity, or you will hear the harshness of unchangeable circumstances and unyielding boxes.

A Formula for Balance Coaching

The formula for moving from stuck to possibility and from possibility to action has five steps: (1) perspectives, (2) choice, (3) co-active strategy, (4) commitment, and (5) action.

Step 1: Perspectives

The first step in balance coaching is to identify the coachee's perspective and then expand the perspectives that are available. It is much harder work to get coachees into action from a stalled or dead-end perspective compared to a perspective that has zoom and flow in it.

As humans, we tend to limit what is possible by what we believe is true, and if a coachee sees a situation as hopeless, it will be very difficult to create the conditions for change. Perception is reality. What's more, the coachee has plenty of evidence from past experience that confirms this view and can tell you with complete certainty that the situation really is a dead end. It's like a lens, formed over time, a filter that only allows the coachee to see things in a certain way. One or two previous experiences with unfortunate results and a perspective is formed—generalized from that sample. Then it becomes a habitual way of thinking. The filter finds more confirming evidence over time until these ways of thinking appear to be true, immutable, obvious. Case closed.

When we take a perspective on an issue, we have an opinion, a belief, assumptions and expectations. It can sound like, "As everyone knows, . . . " or "Trust me; that's the way it works around here." We make predictions based on the assumptions that belong to that perspective. We believe we can predict the outcome because "that's how things always go." Confronted with contrary evidence not explained by the perspective, the objection is invalid or simply dismissed out of hand.

Balance coaching starts by observing that there is a limiting perspective, and then naming it and exploring the impact of holding it. Once we've identified it, we can work with coachees to develop alternative perspectives that are more resourceful and creative and will provide more action possibilities.

You can generate more perspectives by simply asking coachees *What is another way of looking at this that would work for you?* You can also brainstorm metaphors or images that provide creative material for additional perspectives. For example, *How would a five-year-old see this?* or *What is the "good news" perspective?* Or choose one of the coachee's values: *Adventure is a value of yours. What if you looked at this as a grand adventure?*

Geography

Imagine placing an object in the middle of a room—a sculpture of some kind, for instance. Now imagine walking around that object, looking at it from a variety of angles. Each perspective would give you a little more information about the object. Working with perspectives has that effect. But it is much more than just a visual difference as we shift from perspective to perspective. What we discover is that each perspective is a world of its own, with a different landscape, a different climate, and different rules for expected behavior. What might be normal in one perspective/ world is not normal in another.

When we explore the conditions within a perspective with coachees, we are looking at the geography of that world. There is a native language in that perspective. There will be cultural rules and well-formed roles— certain things are permitted and encouraged; others are taboo or simply not possible. There will also be a posture to that perspective, sometimes quite literally, because people embody the perspective they are in and carry it physically, in their bodies.

Consider this perspective: "A walk in the woods is a glorious embrace of the natural world." There is a tone in the language. You can practically smell the fragrance and hear the natural sounds of that perspective. And if you allowed your body to represent that perspective, your posture would incorporate its inherent attitude and beliefs; it would show up in how you stand, what you do with your arms, the tilt of your head. Now notice how dramatically all of that changes with a different perspective. Consider this: "A walk in the woods is a dangerous, messy, bug-ridden, slimy waste of time." See how the tone changes. Body posture changes to reflect the attitude, beliefs, and expectations. Even the smell is different.

These are simply two perspectives on a walk in the woods. Neither is right or wrong, although those who advocate for one or the other no doubt have strong (in their minds), compelling reasons to support their point of view and are prepared to insist very persuasively that their perspective is the right one, the one that is true.

The Topic Is . . .

The example of a walk in the woods also highlights the importance of having a clear topic with the perspective. You need a specific, identifiable topic for consideration, like the sculpture you imagined placing in the middle of a room. The topic could be a situation, a decision that must be made, an event, or a category of events. It could be a contemplated action or an opportunity. It could be a relationship with another person or a relationship between the coachee and something specific, such as a debt, cancer, or technology.

Note that it is easier to work with perspectives when the topic is more specific, even if it is a relationship. The topic itself is neither positive nor negative. In fact, it must be neutral or there is an implied perspective. The coachee's reaction to the topic reveals a perspective. And it is the perspective that brings emotion or judgment.

Step 2: Choice

Playing with perspectives involves exploring the rich territory in each land of the geographic map. You might have a coachee stand in different parts of the room and embody the different perspectives, trying on each one like a costume, getting a feel for the atmosphere and language. Eventually, the coachee will need to choose a perspective—one of the perspectives you have been playing with, a combination of perspectives, or even an entirely new perspective that came out of the exploration.

In our formula, "choice" is more than deciding which perspective to choose. "Choice" at this step is also an affirmation of the power of choice itself. To be aware that there are real and distinct possibilities to choose from is liberating and empowering. Coachees are no longer victims of circumstances over which they have no control. They are agents of personal change—absolutely, unequivocally in charge of their choices.

How coachees choose will also be a revealing part of the process for coachee and coach. Does the coachee choose quickly? Impulsively? Is there a great deal of analysis or a complex system for comparing and analyzing? This information will be valuable background for you as you learn how your coachees typically handle the decision-making process.

This can be especially revelatory for leaders and managers. By observing how coachees make decisions, managers gain great insight into team member performance and each person's role on the team. This insight can lead to more effective team interaction or uncover the need for skills training or development; it can help identify future leadership potential or possibly the lack of a good fit. Such insight is invaluable for leaders.

Step 3: Co-active Strategy

In our approach to balance coaching, this step forms a bridge between awareness and action. A co-active strategy recognizes that moving into action is about more than new activity. A strategy in the co-active model includes the attitude and emotional state that motivates and supports action.

Consistent with the principle of balance, we begin by expanding the range of possibilities so that the action choice comes from a place that is alive. We open up possibilities to create variety and a range of action options. This is an intentionally expansive phase that emphasizes creativity. The skill of brainstorming is one way of generating ideas and options, but no matter what form the creative process takes, the coach's job is to encourage coachees to push the edge of possibilities, to travel beyond familiar alternatives. In this expansion mode, the intention is to redefine what "possible" means, outside the old boundaries and past what is normally considered "realistic." Noting here that "realistic" is a perspective and could be a self-limiting way of looking at the situation at hand.

We make a distinction between discussing a plan and creating a strategy. When this step in the process is based on exploring possibilities rather than navigating around circumstances, it leads to new territory, uncharted opportunities. The circumstances are real; this is not about pretending they don't exist. It is about looking beyond the foreground walls and fences and invoking creative vision.

Given the rich and expanded world of possible actions, the next phase in the process is to narrow the list. This is the next choice point in balance coaching, and it presents an opportunity to make sure, again, that the course of action being considered will lead to more flow.

One of the things to watch for is a condition we playfully call "OOPS": Overly Optimistic Planning Syndrome. Yes, we encourage creating an abundance of possibilities, and we help coachees build a motivational fire that powers their move into action. But we do this to expand the range, not to overburden and cause burnout in our coachees, so checking in and consciously choosing are important parts of creating a co-active strategy. We are looking for a point of balance between abundant possibilities and choices that result in flow.

Ultimately, it is our goal to make sure that there is movement in the issues that are the focus of the coaching session. Narrowing the action list is the step that moves us from conversation into reality. In coaching, it is not enough to have really good—even profound or wildly creative—talk about coachees' issues, circumstances, and perspectives. It is essential that coachees be in action and that something is made real in the world that they can see and take note of. (The Co-Active Online Toolkit includes a variety of strategy and planning tools. *coactive.com/toolkit.*)

Step 4: Commitment

One of the core questions for coaches is *What is it that sustains change over time?* It's so easy to slip back into old habits. Once a new direction is chosen—moving out of the comfort zone of familiar and well-conditioned belief—what will sustain coachees on their way? The energy of commitment is one answer.

Beyond Choice

Strategizing, even in the co-active way, can be just another cerebral activity. The emphasis is on thinking about different ways to make things happen, how to allocate resources, calculating the pros and cons of alternative action steps. The strategy can become an intellectual exercise and feel mechanical to the coachee. As a coach, you want this awakened strategy to live inside, in the coachee's muscle and bone, not only in the brain. So before you invite coachees to take action, make sure they've really made a commitment to their plans.

People gain a mysterious strength and resolve when they make a commitment. Commitment goes beyond making a choice. We make a choice between lasagna and linguine; we make a commitment to other people, to life, to a course of action. Commitment implies there is no turning back. This is the point where you draw a line and ask the coachee to cross into new territory: *Will you commit to that plan and take action? Will you do that?* Up to this point, coachees may simply have been playing along. Chances are that they will experience a shift once they realize that they are committing to a different way of operating in their world. And so you ask, *Will you commit to this plan?*

This question raises the stakes. We're no longer talking about losing 10 pounds or paying down the credit card balance or finishing the spreadsheet with sales targets for the third quarter. We're talking about coachees taking control of the choices in their lives. Each of these action steps is connected at a deeper level when it is anchored in commitment. In fact, this act of commitment is so powerful that the coach sometimes asks coachees to actually draw a line—real or imaginary—on the floor in front of them, take a deep breath, and, when they're ready to commit to the plan, step across the line. But only when they're truly ready to commit.

Yes and No

The words *yes* and *no* are two of the simplest words in any language. Depending on the context of the question, however, they can also be two of the most difficult words to say out loud for the whole world to hear. As coachees prepare to commit to action, they must choose between saying yes to their plans and saying no to something else.

In the context of commitment, those words have a deeper ring; they reverberate into your coachee's life. That yes to a simple action is a yes to some deeper commitment, a self-promise. Saying no to a simple action is much more than taking that one thing off the list. It often means saying no to old beliefs or expectations, no to self-betrayal, no to habitual ways of reacting to the demands of others.

As coach, listen for the depth of the yeses and nos from your coachees. You may even ask them to take part in this yes-or-no exercise for a period of time as a way to get clearer about the root choices they are making. For example: *In your life these days, what are you saying yes to? What are you saying no to?* or *In your relationship with your spouse, what are you saying yes to or no to?* or *For your role in this organization, what are you saying yes to? What are you saying no to?*

Step 5: Action

The action of coaching does not take place in the coaching session. From the coach's point of view, this is something of a relief. It eliminates the pressure to be brilliant or perfect or transformative. The real action of coaching takes place in the coachee's life, in the action he or she takes— or doesn't take—between sessions. That is where the power is. Without action, the balance coaching is incomplete, just an enjoyable conversation about point of view. Action steps in the coachee's life keep the coachee moving and motivated.

At the next session, you will check in on progress, explore what worked and what didn't, and go over what the coachee learned from both. You will uncover what this person wants to take into his or her life from here, as he or she balances circumstances and possibilities and makes life-giving choices in action.

For leaders and managers, the follow-up will likely be informal, but it will be just as important. Taking action without harvesting the learning is merely activity or busyness. Exploring the learning is what leads to individual development and meaningful results. Balance coaching is a way, a process that trains people to see everyday action in a bigger context.

Sample Dialogue

> **MANAGER (after listening to the direct report's discouraged update on a particular project):** I'm guessing you thought you would be much more excited about the project than you are.

> **Direct Report:** That's an understatement. I thought this was going to be the creative crème de la crème.

> **MANAGER:** And it's not.

> **Direct Report:** Nope. Definitely not crème de la anything. Oatmeal, I'd say. Day-old oatmeal.

MANAGER: Sounds like you're up to your hips in this day-old oatmeal.

Direct Report: Yeah, I'm not going anywhere fast. With half the people pulled off the project for other things—and a dotted-line project manager who is not at all invested in making this a priority—it's discouraging.

MANAGER: So there you are in the oatmeal perspective, looking at the project. Let's play with this for a bit. What's the air like in that perspective?

Direct Report: Air? Stale. Old. Rank.

MANAGER: Hard to get very motivated from this place.

Direct Report: I'll say.

MANAGER: Want to try looking at it in a different way?

Direct Report: Sure. Anything's got to be an improvement.

MANAGER: So, what would a different perspective be?

Direct Report: Well, it could be summer vacation. You know, school's out, no more teachers, no more books.

MANAGER: Good. What's the theme in this perspective?

Direct Report: Freedom. I can do anything I want.

MANAGER: Okay. Just so we can keep track of these as we go along, let's draw a circle and divide it into eight wedges—like pie slices. Put "oatmeal" in one of those wedges, then select one of the other wedges and put "school's out" in that one. Got it?

Direct Report: Yes.

MANAGER: What would be another perspective?

Direct Report: I'm not sure.

MANAGER: What's something you love to do?

Direct Report: I have a workshop at home where I do simple woodwork projects. It's a hobby. It relaxes me. I like working with my hands.

MANAGER: Sounds like you have a clear sense of this perspective.

Direct Report: Oh yeah. I can practically smell the wood.

MANAGER: What shall we call this one?

Direct Report: Just call it workshop—it's creative and satisfying and useful.

MANAGER: What's another way you could look at this project?

[The Coachee finds a couple more perspectives, including one he labels "library." Coach and Coachee explore the characteristics of the different perspectives.]

MANAGER: Looking at my notes, I see that we've talked about six, seven if you include the original oatmeal perspective. Which is the one you will choose?

Direct Report: The library.

MANAGER: And what is there about the library perspective that appeals to you?

Direct Report: Well, I wish this project was up and running full-speed with this really hot, creative team together. We talked about that, but it's not going to happen in the short term. What would be interesting, though, is to really go in and study the subject. I've got the time. I like the library as a metaphor because it's a quiet place. It's set aside for study, and there's lots of material to explore. No one's going to bother me there.

MANAGER: Great. So now that you're standing in the library looking at the project, what are some of the options? What might you be doing with your time?

Direct Report: There's some online research I'd like to do . . . two books I've been meaning to order . . . I just haven't done it. And there's a guy in Ireland I'd like to talk to. He's involved in a similar project—we chatted by email a few months back . . . There's also a conference coming up in a couple of months—I suppose I could see if the company would fund my trip . . .

MANAGER: Lots of options. What would be the stretch for you?

Direct Report: Writing an article on the subject would be a stretch.

MANAGER: And what would you be saying yes to?

Direct Report: I'd be saying yes to taking control of my time. I'd be saying yes to capitalizing on the opportunity. I'd be saying yes to making this downtime a real benefit to me in my career—being willing to be a colleague of sorts, with some of the people I admire—earning my professional credentials, so to speak.

MANAGER: And what would you be saying no to?

Direct Report: Well, the obvious. No to whining and complaining that I don't get to play the way I expected. But more than that, I'd be saying no to that weary sense of helplessness.

MANAGER: How committed are you to writing this article?

Direct Report: Very. This should be really interesting—and it leads to all sorts of other possibilities.

MANAGER: Good. What would lock in this sense of commitment for you?

Direct Report: Committing to some kind of action step.

MANAGER: I was just about to ask. What do you want to be accountable for, and what would the stretch timeline be for that action step?

Direct Report: An outline would be the next step. I would need to do some of the research I talked about—at least a quick look at some things—and I know what that would be. I could have a draft of an outline in, say, two weeks.

MANAGER: All right, then. Here's my request: Send me a copy of the outline on that day. Will you do that?

Direct Report: Let me put that in my calendar. Okay, I'll do it.

Finding the Balance

The purpose of the balance formula, and balance coaching for that matter, is to move coachees into action. Like a slalom skier speeding down the mountain, turning crisply at every chute, we live our lives in action, and being on the edge is an exhilarating way to experience life in motion. If the image of the skier and the mountain is a little too breathtaking for your taste, the same themes apply to the ice-skater and the dancer. Grace and performance also demonstrate the balance point of leaning into what is possible while still maintaining control.

And yet, we are not assisting our coachees with just any action. It's not a service to coachees to simply add more action to their lives. Fulfillment coaching will help identify action that is consistent with the coachee's values. Balance coaching will help coachees choose the flow, a way to balance priorities, expectations, and perspectives on the issues they bring to their coaching sessions. Our use of the word *flow* isn't meant to imply glassy smoothness. You may want to substitute the word *ride* for *flow* because our goal is to help coachees create the ride of their life. The action coachees undertake by working from the principle of balance is action that fits the big-picture ride that brings them a life of choice.

CHAPTER 10

Process

Coachees usually come to coaching to do things differently or to do different things. They want to set goals, come up with plans, get into action, and use the accountability of coaching to stay on track. Coachees want to be in motion, not standing still, so naturally a great deal of the coach's focus is on moving forward, helping coachees envision the golden future and the path that will take them there. There is a leaning-forward, feet-moving, arms-pumping quality to the coaching. And yet, in co-active coaching, we believe there is more to life than tasks accomplished. Our focus is on the coachee's life experience, not just a list of action items completed. In fact, we believe coachees actually want to enjoy the journey, to savor and appreciate each moment of their lives as best they can.

In general, fulfillment and balance focus on moving forward. Coach and coachee are aware of what is happening externally in the coachee's life, and they can see the results. Coaching that emphasizes moving forward is focused, directed, intentional. It is about generating, creating. Action orientation often has a fierce determination to make something happen— coachees are looking ahead, and there is momentum.

Process coaching focuses on the internal experience, on what is happening in the moment. The goal of process coaching is to enhance the ability of coachees to be aware of the moment and to name it. In process coaching, there is a quality of expanding into the present, being curious about it, slowing down to explore and appreciate it. Sometimes the most important change happens at the internal level and may even be necessary before external change can take place. Being in the moment immerses the coachee in the flow of life, the here and now. The feeling is expansive, like going up a mountain to a higher place or down into the valley to a deeper place.

The combination of going somewhere and going more deeply into the experience is the full spectrum of life. Being present in life expands awareness, leads to richer highs and robust lows that are the measure of a true life fully experienced. This is the process-coaching version of the coachee's big agenda: a fully expressed and fully experienced life lived in the moment.

The Look of Process

Process coaching focuses on where coachees are now. Imagine life as a river, flowing through time. In one place, the river is steady, serene. Then it hits the rapids. Then a waterfall. There are eddies and whirlpools, back-water and swamps. The river of life narrows and suddenly speeds up. Process is about being fully aware and alive wherever you are on the river today: whether you are floating easily on your back, enjoying the sky and sun, or tumbling through the chaos of white water.

Coachees have their plans and dreams, and sometimes they won't like where they are on the river. And yet, when you're in the rapids, the only thing to do is be in the rapids. You can wish it weren't so, but that's where you are. While you are busy making plans for the future, you are also in the present. You are in the process of your life. In this moment. Right now.

The Coach and Process

Imagine the river on a bright afternoon. The sun reflecting off the water in glittering sparkles can be practically blinding. As with the river, it's easy to be distracted by the activity on the surface of life. Action can be dazzling. But when you look at the river through a polarizing filter, you tune out the distracting sparkles and see the flow of the water. That's the coach's job—to notice the currents below the surface. In process coaching, you are tuning your ear to hear below the surface, noticing anything stirring that feels out of place, inconsistent, something like resistance or an unexpected turbulence. It is a signal to you that there is an undercurrent that is likely obstructing the flow of the river. You can hear it by listening attentively at Level III, and as a coach, you become curious. Very often it is something the coachee is not conscious of or is avoiding.

Process Coaching

Ultimately, our goal as coaches is to assist our coachees in creating the work and lives they want. In a sense, we are always focused on moving forward to an envisioned future. However, the shortest distance between here and there is not always a straight line. Sometimes it is a curved line, as the U-shaped process pathway shows (see figure 6). Sometimes the way forward involves going down into the experience first. Or, as we will see a little later, it may mean going up into the experience first, by simply turning the U-shaped curve upside down.

The flow in process coaching has the following steps: (1) the coach senses the turbulence under the surface and names it, (2) the coach explores it, (3) the coachee experiences it, (4) a shift happens, (5) energy opens up, (6) the coachee has access to new resources, and (7) movement happens.

1: The Coach Senses Turbulence under the Surface and Names It

Listening at Level III, you as coach sense there is something unnamed under the surface of the coaching conversation. You can feel the unexpressed emotion; it's blocked, pent up, being held in check, managed. Process coaching draws on the coach's ability to be aware of these emotional undercurrents—they are a crucial part of the coaching conversation, too; they reveal information about what is important to coachees. The energy of the emotion is a flashing sign—sometimes dimly flashing, sometimes brightly flashing.

For example, a coachee could be describing a change in departmental policies at work, and underneath the words, there is barely controlled outrage, a fire-breathing dragon, burned by the injustice of the way the new policies were introduced. At this point, you become curious. Clearly, something very important is going on just below the surface—something more important than the policies themselves—it's about the impact of this experience on the coachee. It can happen the opposite way, too: You expect your coachee to be euphoric about a recent success, but the

1. Coach hears the turbulence and names it

2. Coach explores it

7. Movement happens

3. Client experiences it

6. Client has access to new resources

5. Energy opens up

4. A shift happens

FIGURE 6   The Process Pathway

coachee's voice and tone are dead flat. That's another good reason to become curious.

When the coach hears it, he or she speaks or names it—and invites the coachee to look there, too. In relation to the examples we gave, this means that you, the coach, share your observation, without judgment or attachment. It can be as simple as saying, "It sounds to me like there's something important here about the way you were treated." Or you could be more specific, especially in ongoing coach-coachee relationships, such as, "That's not the outcome you hoped for. It sounds like you're really disappointed."

We invite coachees to look below the surface, below the facts and data. Why would we do this? The most powerful, most effective coaching we can do always works with what is most important for the coachee.

When you point below the surface to the energy or emotion, you give the coachee an opportunity to learn more about what is obviously important. Coachees are not always prepared to look below the surface; they often keep their emotional responses under tight control. By inviting your coachees to explore the energy or emotion around the subject, you give them the opportunity to become aware and conscious of the impact these issues really have on their lives.

Coachees aren't the only ones who are reluctant to look below the surface—coaches are, too. Where fulfillment has vision and values to make meaningful choices, and balance has action and planning, process can feel like vast territory without a map or compass. And it might get emotional and messy. Where balance relies on commitment, process relies on trust. In fact, not only is process coaching built on trust, but it also builds trust. As coaches we ask coachees to be open, willing to explore, to trust the process. The same applies to those who coach.

This can be a particularly sensitive subject for managers and leaders. Emotions at work are often seen as problematic—to be avoided or handled with extreme care. We might wish that all employee contact was thoughtful and easily managed, and that the coaching interactions would all comfortably lead to clear action and valuable learning, but there are times when the most important thing to deal with in the moment is the emotional context because it is so present. After all, humans come with emotion. It's actually a sign of life. Imagine a workplace that was completely sterile, devoid of emotion. The good news? Process coaching in the co-active way gives leaders and managers tools that support team members in those moments.

Managers who become more skillful at navigating emotional waters create an environment where it is safe to be fully human, fully present. This is a culture that has the strength and range to include the highs and the lows that are normal in life. Employees feel known and seen as people—not just functions.

2: The Coach Explores It

Once you have heard and named the turbulence, the next step is to explore the territory—but first you must ask the coachee for permission. This is important. With some coachees, especially in an ongoing coaching relationship, you will find you have great latitude to take them into whatever territory you, as an experienced coach, feel would be most beneficial for them. These coachees have granted permission broadly and empowered you to take the lead in deciding where the coaching conversation needs to go. With other coachees, especially those relatively new to coaching or to you as a coach, asking permission creates a container of safety and encourages them to look deeper than the surface details of the presenting issue.

For managers it's especially important to ask permission. It's both responsible and respectful of the other person's feelings in the moment. People can feel vulnerable, and the presence of emotion often feels awkward or unsafe. Simply noticing the obvious—that there is something more going on than the topic itself—and asking if it's okay to talk about it, creates a co-active peer relationship where the employee is in control. Both "yes" and "no, not now" are legitimate responses.

The goal of process coaching, as we have said, is to focus on what is true in the moment. One of the most effective access points for exploring the moment is the coachee's immediate physical experience: breathing, tension, a furrowed brow, tightness in the throat, or a rapid heartbeat. The body is remarkably expressive, and it is a rich source of information about the coachee's internal experience.

Metaphor or imagery is another effective access point for exploring the moment. Sometimes the feelings are easier to describe in pictures than in words: *The feeling is a small tight ball . . . The feeling is a helium-filled Mylar balloon . . . It feels like walking through waist-deep mud . . . It feels like flying around and around and around in a little circle.*

3: The Coachee Experiences It

The key here is that the coachee actually experience the sensation or emotion. It is important for the coachee to be able to name it and identify it, even if only in a few words, but just talking about it will not usually be enough to shift the feeling. As coach, you can tell the difference between a conversation about disappointment and a coachee who is reliving the experience of disappointment. An intellectual understanding of what caused the disappointment is a good start, but there is much deeper learning available.

4: A Shift Happens

There is a moment when we can feel a change in the tide. There we were, going more deeply into the energy and emotion of an experience, and then it shifted. The air, the tone, the light, the weight—it's hard to find the right words for it, but it is a sensation of new movement. We are no longer diving; we are rising.

We have drawn the graphic of process coaching as a very tidy U-shaped curve, but a coaching session that followed that ideal path would be a near miracle. Most of the time, if you were to graph the movement, you would see that the coaching goes deeper, resurfaces slightly, plateaus perhaps, goes deeper again, and so on. There is no perfect template for process coaching because the coach is constantly dancing in the moment with each new response. And yet, listening at Level III, there is almost always a point in time when, as coach, you can hear the coachee rising up the far side of the U-shaped curve.

5. Energy Opens Up

The shift is accompanied by a sense of opening, release, expansion. Emotion has powerful energy in it. When that emotion is blocked, the energy builds behind the walls, sometimes driven down and pressed into corners. Process coaching unblocks that stuck energy and allows the energy of the emotion to serve the coachee. Unblocked energy creates motion. The motion of process feels quite different from fulfillment or balance because it draws on the coachee's emotional energy working under the surface. In this way emotion becomes energy in motion: "e-motion" for the coachee. Process is about being with what is true, and sometimes the emotion is what is most true for the coachee and the means for forward motion.

6. Coachee Has New Resources

Managing, controlling, and suppressing the emotion takes effort; it expends internal resources. Once the shift happens and coachees find they are in new, more expansive territory, they also have access to more of their own internal resources. Those resources for making life-giving choices were always there—this isn't acquiring new resources—it's the experience of releasing that energy for the work that matters most to coachees. Coachees are more energized to take on the tasks, even the battles, necessary to move forward in their lives.

7: Movement Happens

In this step, there is a sense that movement is underway, that we have entered a new phase. The atmosphere changes. Coachees may describe the experience as feeling more buoyant or seeing the situation in new, brighter, or more colorful light. They may report a sensation of warmth or more flow, or say they are more relaxed, more at peace or more energized, less stuck or resistant, and so on. In most cases, this new sensation can be linked to a new understanding or awareness in the coachee.

The outcome of process coaching is a shift in the internal experience combined with new or renewed learning. As we said, coaching is about moving forward, and sometimes progress starts with going into the experience, not skipping over it. There is important, sometimes life-changing information in the exploration that emotions signal to coachees and coach. The result is more empowered action and a more resourceful coachee.

Going Up Into It

The steps we've just described apply equally to those situations in which coachees seem reluctant to go "up" into an experience. Coachees can be so driven to move on to the next stage or the next project or challenge that they want to skip the celebration of their accomplishments—and miss the chance to discover more about themselves and the keys to their success.

Some coachees have been told too often and for too long that they need to be humble or should not draw attention to themselves, and so they avoid what they consider self-praise and miss out on acknowledgment and learning. Some coachees are simply afraid of being too happy, or they consider the more joyful emotions unnecessary or a sign that they are not taking the issue seriously.

As a coach, part of your job is to listen for the kind of avoidance that keeps your coachees from experiencing the whole range of musical notes available to them. When coachees cut themselves off from the highs and lows, it's like cutting out musical tones. They end up with only a few notes to play, which makes for a very limited and monotonous life song.

Feelings as Information, Not Symptoms

The presence of feelings or emotions is one of the inherent qualities of process coaching. When coachees talk freely about issues that are deeply important to them, it should come as no surprise that the conversation takes place in an atmosphere of feeling. Coaches are sometimes alarmed and confused by this. They think that because the coachee is reacting with feeling, the coaching relationship has turned into therapy.

But emotions and therapy are not the same. Emotions are just emotions. When people are passionate, even angry, about a perceived injustice, it doesn't mean that they are mentally unstable; they are human beings having a human reaction.

It's okay for coaches to allow emotion—sadness, pain, anger, loss—and actually to encourage it. Emotion is a legitimate form of expression, like words, music, and dance. Don't be a detective about it. Don't look at why the coachee is hurt or angry—which is the typical response. The cause itself is not important; accepting the feeling is important. Nor is it up to the coach to try to heal it or stop it—another typical response. Just explore it and acknowledge it: "That's a powerful feeling. There's some pain in there; I can tell."

Emotions are part of the normal functioning of a human being, not symptoms of disease. The whole, healthy, resourceful coachee has full access to his or her emotions. It's the hiding, denying, submerging that get coachees in trouble. Our feelings give us a way of expressing ourselves. The process can be very cleansing, and if we don't permit our bodies to discharge and discover whatever we're holding inside, we don't grow. We can even get sick—physically and emotionally—by keeping things in.

Notice any tendency in yourself to want to make the emotion go away—out of a desire for the coachee to feel better or because you are uncomfortable with the emotion. Remember that the coachee is naturally creative, resourceful, and whole and does not need to be rescued. Your responsibility is to be present and be supportive.

Process coaching is where emotions will show up because you're encouraging, even challenging, coachees to visit the hard places and go into the experience so they can learn why this is important. If it weren't important there wouldn't be this emotional energy around it. When they do go in, they discover more about themselves and become more resourceful, and they release the energy in the emotion—what we've referred to as "e-motion"—to motivate new movement. Unless you can explore those places with your coachees or coachees, your coaching will lack depth and breadth.

Even though process coaching can be powerful emotionally, there's still room for humor. Exploring forbidden territory with humor can give coachees license to approach the dark areas on light feet or to feel curiosity about the depth of the murky water instead of fearing that they are about to drown.

Coaching is all about change, and change is inherently challenging. No matter how shiny that fulfillment vision is, or the life-giving plan for more balanced choices, change is about new behavior and learning, and in the midst of it coachees are more vulnerable. That's especially true with process coaching because of the context of emotion. The payoff for taking what may feel like a risk is that the vulnerability builds trust. There will be a stronger, more effective relationship built between coach and coachee that will serve the coachee in the future. For leaders and managers, building trust creates more effective relationships within the team and a more bonded and resilient team culture.

Sample Dialogue

Coachee: Looks like I'll have to dust off the old résumé again after all.

COACH: You finally heard about the job overseas?

Coachee: I heard. And it wasn't the answer I wanted to hear. So I'm cranking up the search machinery again.

COACH: You had a lot riding on getting that job. I remember how excited you were after the last interview. Sounds like you're kind of shrugging it off now—as if it wasn't that important. What's the truth there?

Coachee: I've got a decent job and little risk that anything will change there.

COACH: Up until today, that wasn't enough.

Coachee: I know. It's still not. The truth is, I am disappointed.

COACH: Not just a little, it sounds like.

Coachee: No. Really disappointed. I was really pumped for that interview. I don't see how it could have gone any better.

COACH: It's a huge letdown.

Coachee: I don't want to dwell on it.

COACH: I understand. Still, it looks as if your life wants to dwell on it.

Coachee: Boy, that's the truth. I can't remember being this unhappy—not about a job falling through. Maybe I had too much riding on getting the hell out of the country.

COACH: What does it look like to you? I'm sensing sadness. What's your experience?

Coachee: It's actually like getting punched in the stomach. I feel like it took my breath away. Like I can't even stand up straight.

COACH: What's the painful part?

Coachee: The loss, the waiting, the wasted energy.

COACH: Would it be all right if we explored that right now? I think it's important to go through this, not step over it.

Coachee: Sure. I want to get over it so I can get on with my life.

COACH: So what's it like there, right now? The place you got punched?

Coachee: It's dark . . . hollow . . . like a cavern.

COACH: Go into the cavern. Are you there?

Coachee: Yes.

COACH: What are you sensing?

Coachee: I'm sitting with my head in my hands.

COACH: What's the emotion?

Coachee: Sadness. I feel defeated. Utterly defeated.

COACH: Okay. What I want you to do now is turn up the volume on it, just a little at first. If it's at 5 right now, turn it up to 6.

Coachee: The sadness?

COACH: Yes. And the feeling of defeat. Go in there. I'll be right here.

Coachee: Okay. I'm turning up the volume. There's 6.

COACH: What do you notice?

Coachee: A sense of failure. Like a huge wave of failure. It's breaking over everything.

COACH: A wave of failure. Are you in a safe place?

Coachee: Yes.

COACH: When you're ready, try turning it up another notch to 7.

Coachee: Now I really feel the loss. Like a dream died. Like my last chance to build something important just vanished.

COACH: This is important for you.

Coachee: It's huge.

COACH: What do you notice now?

Coachee: That I can turn down the volume.

COACH: Do you want to do that now?

Coachee: I do.

COACH: What does it feel like now?

Coachee: The tension is gone from my shoulders.

COACH: Where are you? Are you still in the cavern?

Coachee: No. I'm sitting on a dock, looking out at the ocean.

COACH: What are you learning from this?

Coachee: A couple of things. One, I didn't realize just how important it was to me, to get that position, and how hard it is on me to not be chosen—especially when I really feel qualified. And two, I see that I do control my destiny and how I feel about it, just like I controlled the feeling of failure. I can choose to feel good about myself.

COACH: What's next?

Coachee: The résumé. I do want to work on that some. And I want to go back and do some research into possible overseas work opportunities.

COACH: Good. Sometime this week, create a plan with deadlines and send me a copy. Okay?

Coachee: Okay.

COACH: I also have a request—a homework inquiry—that you spend some time journaling about this theme: "What I have learned from failure." Will you do that?

Coachee: Are you kidding?

COACH: Actually, I'm not kidding. You know how to do whatever you need to do in the job search—write a résumé, do the interviews, whatever needs to be done. The hard thing for you is to live with the feeling of failure. The very prospect could derail you. If you could have more capacity to be with failure, what would it give you?

Coachee: Freedom. It would turn failure into learning instead of judgment about me. It's just . . . I don't have to be happy about doing this, do I?

COACH: You get to choose, as you said just a minute ago. It's just that this won't be the last time you'll face this sense of loss and failure. If you can be with it now—and develop some muscles to handle it—you'll be in better shape the next time you're in a situation like this.

Coachee: Like an emotional fitness program.

COACH: Something like that. And the universe has just provided a great gymnasium for you. Let's take advantage of it.

Process and Accountability

The co-active coaching model is very clear: the coach brings a context to the coaching relationship that includes deepened learning and action that moves the coachee forward in life. Accountability is just as important in process coaching as it is in fulfillment or balance coaching. Without accountability, coaching has not happened, even if coaching skills have been used. The action of coaching takes place in the coachee's life.

With process coaching, the action is designed to support what the coachee discovers from the coaching session. For example, the session might uncover the coachee's fear of disappointing others when he says no to requests. In this case, the coachee is paying a heavy price to avoid the possibility of disappointing people. The accountability might be to risk disappointing people by saying no five times in the coming week and noticing what happens. Or it could also be a habit or practice that is integrated into the coachee's life, such as recording, at the end of each day, the times when he said no and the impact he noticed.

To Be With

A word or two is in order about the expression "be with," which is often used with process coaching. We might say, for example, that coachees are "being with" disappointment, or the coach is "being with" coachees and their disappointment. Think of it like visiting a friend in the hospital. Your goal is to be with your friend. There is really nothing for you to do except to be there. And it is more than just showing up. To be with is to be present and fully engaged, attentive, open, even interacting, but with no goal other than simply being together with that person in the experience. Being with is a powerful Level III environment—an experience shared at a deep level. When you are with coachees at this level, they are free to share not only their thoughts and analyses but the honest emotions of their experiences as well.

Can't Go There

Process coaching often shows up when the river takes a turn into territory the coachee doesn't want to enter. As a coach, your curiosity is piqued. Where is it the coachee doesn't want to go? What is it the coachee doesn't want to deal with? You may hear any number of explanations: "I don't want any more chaos or judgment," "I don't want to worry about money," "I can't be with the failure I created in my last job," "I can't be with the happiness this person brings to my life."

Coachees are uncomfortable—sometimes downright miserable—because their lives are taking them to places where they do not want to go. Coachees in this situation want to change course and avoid those areas. What they get, over time, are lives filled with avoiding. They don't realize what it costs them to cut out those parts of their lives. To demonstrate this idea, draw a large circle to represent the coachee's whole life (see figure 7). Ask the coachee, "What's one thing that's hard to be with? Let's exclude

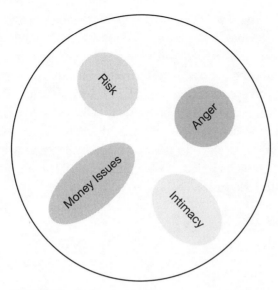

FIGURE 7   Redirecting the Flow

that from the picture." Draw a small shape inside the circle and give it a name, and continue that process. Mark off the pieces the coachee doesn't want to be with. Color the pieces in and name them: this is the anger the coachee can't be with . . . the disappointment . . . the risk taking. As each piece is colored in, there is less life left for the coachee, and it becomes harder and harder to navigate around all the "don't go there" zones.

Process coaching helps coachees develop the capacity to be with conditions they have been denying or avoiding. Much of our work as coaches is helping coachees discover what is true, real, and important, so that they can choose well. We could also say that our job is to help coachees stop avoiding, pretending, denying. From this empowered place, they will be able to make better decisions and be stronger in their relationships at work and at home.

Where Do You Stop?

Before we leave the subject of exploring the hard places, we should ask a pointed question: *What areas in your life are hard for you to be with or explore?* The answer is important because these are the places you'll be reluctant to go to with your coachees. You might even stop in your coaching rather than get into these places. Let's say you have trouble dealing with money, or anger, or rejection. You may avoid these areas in your coaching. Yet these may be the places your coachees need and are even willing to explore. If you are not conscious of your own off-limits areas, you'll shortchange your coachees, because as soon as they start to go there, you'll steer them away. Coaches, therefore, must do their own rigorous process of self-discovery—ideally with their own coach. Begin to work on these areas so they can be included in your own life and become accessible in your work with coachees, too.

PART 4

Integration and Vision

Atypical coaching session has a familiar, energetic flow to it. The first phase of the conversation is expansive. Doors are opening. Avenues are being explored. At some point the arc begins to turn downward, like coming over a hill, and there is a gathering energy that carries us toward completion. You can feel the momentum building. The pace changes; the conversation takes on a more directional feel. We are focusing in and moving to a conclusion: a choice, a decision, a commitment.

In coaching, that "finish line" is not an end point. It's a new beginning point for action. The journey continues. Vistas open up and the road stretches toward the horizon.

As this book comes to completion, a similar energy flow is pulling us forward. We've explored the model, the contexts, and the principles; we have practiced the skills and sampled the dialogue in the framework of professional coaching, in the informal coaching role of leaders and managers, and in co-active conversations generally. In these last two chapters, we integrate the work we've discussed and then pause to envision what is possible from here.

CHAPTER 11

Putting It All Together

So far, we have spoken of the three core principles as distinct pathways of coaching. In separating them for the book, we may have left an impression that a coaching session follows one consistent principle from first question to final accountability. In fact, in the course of a single coaching session, you, as coach, are likely to weave together elements of all three principles: fulfillment, balance, and process.

Integrating the Principles

We might think of the three principles as three different sets of tools. When coach and coachee explore values, a future vision, or the self-sabotage that can keep coachees from achieving their vision, the coach is pulling from the fulfillment toolkit. When the coach helps coachees look at an issue from a variety of different viewpoints or consider plans or action options, the toolkit is balance-based. The coach who forms a container around the current moment and delves more deeply into it is in the general area of process. So how do you, as coach, decide which tool set to begin with? And how do you recognize that it is time to shift to a different principle? The short answer is that the coaching direction comes from listening at Levels II and III.

As we have said from the outset, in the co-active coaching model, the goals and focus areas for the coaching, and the issues for any given coaching session, come from the coachee. Coachees set the agenda for the coaching relationship and each coaching session. That is their responsibility.

It is the coach's responsibility to determine what coaching approach to take. The coachee is actually counting on the coach to take charge of the coaching direction and flow. The coach chooses a direction beginning with the coachee's very first statement in the session. In our listening model, we say that the coach is paying attention to the coachee, aware of the strength of the one-to-one connection; this is what we describe as listening at Level II. The coach is also paying attention to the coachee's shifting tone, the pace of speaking or breathing, and the atmosphere that is created. The coach is even gauging the strength of the relationship itself: is the coachee moving closer, drifting away, running away, defending? This is the coach listening at Level III.

For the coach, the information about where to go next with the coaching is right there, in the moment, in the Level II and Level III listening. This is crucial for coaches working in this model. Coaches listen for an overall sense of movement or energy and use that information to help form the next question or decide which skill to apply next.

This is definitely an art that requires attentive listening and then dancing with whatever shows up. It is not a technique to be learned, as in "When the coachee says *A*, then the coach asks *B*." It doesn't work that way. It also doesn't work for you, as coach, to have your attention on the tool set, thinking about which principle you are working in, which context of the model you are using, or what skill to pick from the glossary. That is awareness at Level I, and when you are at this level, you have disconnected from the coachee. It happens to the best coaches from time to time, and coaches then need to recover and reconnect to the coachee.

Notice we have specifically said *reconnect to the coachee* rather than *reconnect to the coachee's issue*. In coaching, our primary responsibility is to help coachees determine their best course of action and support them in staying on track, helping them uncover the learning for themselves so that they become more resourceful over time rather than more dependent on the coach for answers. As coaches, we are always empowering our coachees.

This urge to identify the "problem" as quickly as possible and find a solution in the blink of an eye is embedded in the culture. Yes, of course there are times when it is crucial to solve problems quickly, but in coaching, we take a longer view of coachees and their lives. In our model of coaching, coaches are holding the coachee's big agenda: a resonant, fulfilling life—a life of choice and purpose and expression. We help coachees look at the issues they bring to coaching within a larger context.

For coaches, it is a professional hazard to be seduced into wanting to understand all of the circumstances around a coachee's issue, as if our understanding would make us better equipped to help our coachees. In almost every case, we overestimate what we need to know. After all, coachees are the experts on their own lives and work situations; the coach is the expert in helping them find the next course of action and reap the learning from the action they take.

We should note here that there is no superficial coachee issue, only superficial coaching. There is always something important underneath the situation presented, or it would not be worth the coachee's or the coach's time. Part of the coach's job is to look for whatever makes an issue important in a coachee's life.

Every presenting issue in coaching has within it the potential to move the coachee closer to his or her version of fulfillment, balance, or better process in life. The issue that a coachee brings is a piece of a much larger puzzle. It should be treated with respect, not as a problem to be solved so that it disappears but rather as an opportunity to move toward a larger goal. In the end, this is the real leverage of coaching: not an answer to a single issue, but a more empowered and resourceful coachee living a more alive and rewarding life.

This urge to address the problem or give advice is particularly tempting—habit-forming, you might say—for leaders and managers. That's how the role has been defined for them for generations. Taking a "coach-approach" is new, unfamiliar, and maybe even uncomfortable territory. The process is not very clear—certainly not as simple as giving the "right" answer—and the outcome is somewhat elusive, as in, "What's the point? I can see it's a nail, plain as day, and I have a hammer—and I know how to use it." The opportunity to support the development of more skilled "carpenters" for the sake of the team and organization needs to be emphasized.

That awareness provides a larger lens for the conversation between manager and direct report. Instead of a microscopic and short-term effect, there is the breadth and depth possible from a selection of the three core principles woven together to give employees more access to a valued life at work: a life that is in action and balance and open to being present in the process.

Sample Coaching

Integrating the Three Principles Dialogue

Coachee: Picking up where we left off last time . . . I'm still playing with the possibility of buying the business I talked about.

COACH: You've been gathering data . . .

Coachee: . . . And I talked to the broker again.

COACH: As you view this potential acquisition, where are you today? What's the big picture? [Vision: fulfillment]

Coachee: The big picture is, it's risky.

COACH: I notice "risky" hasn't stopped you before. In fact, risk taking is a big value of yours. What is there about this risk that's different? [Values: fulfillment]

Coachee: It's complex.

COACH: Let's try to pull it apart a little. First of all, I trust you have a way to make sure the financial picture makes sense to you.

Coachee: I'm going to go over all of that with my partner and the CPA we've been working with, but basically, the analysis is handled. By this time next week, we'll know everything we need to know.

COACH: So there is some financial risk. Is that the risky part?

Coachee: Not really. I'm familiar with spreadsheets, and I can make a solid business decision based on the numbers.

COACH: So what is at risk here?

Coachee: You remember that theme we talked about, the theme for this year? My slowing down.

COACH: "Getting off the highway," I think, was the way you expressed it.

Coachee: Well, if I decide to buy this business, it won't be "getting off the highway"; it will be "moving into the fast lane."

COACH: Your voice just shifted there. What happened? [In the moment: process]

Coachee: I can feel the pressure building.

COACH: What's the feeling? [Being with: process]

Coachee: A sense of dread.

COACH: What sort of image comes to mind when you let yourself feel the dread?

Coachee: I get all hunched over at the shoulders, like I'm carrying a heavy weight.

COACH: That's what it feels like when you look at the decision through the lens of "moving into the fast lane." What if you could look at this acquisition through the lens of your theme, "getting off the highway"? What would that be like? [Perspectives: balance]

Coachee: That would be a stretch.

COACH: Want to try it?

Coachee: Sure.

[Coach and coachee explore this and several other perspectives.]

COACH: What are you taking away from the coaching today?

Coachee: Two things: one, that I can handle the financial analysis, and two, the financial analysis is only one part of the decision. What's really important is how this decision impacts my life. I see that I get addicted to the excitement of making a deal and can lose track of what's really important to me in the long run.

COACH: I have a homework inquiry for you to reflect on. Ready?

Coachee: Yes.

COACH: What is the payoff you most want from this potential acquisition? [Big agenda: fulfillment]

Coachee: That's good. I'll take that on.

Wearing Multiple Hats

What happens when the coach really *does* have expertise that would be valuable to coachees? It seems unfair, maybe even unprofessional, to hold back information or experience that could save coachees from making costly mistakes or that could simply help them cut through a long and wandering learning process. The key in this situation is to be clear on several different levels.

> First, ask yourself, *Is the information I have truly relevant to the coachee and the coachee's situation? What specifically will this coachee gain from my contribution?*

> Second, be clear with yourself and your coachee that you are not wearing your coach's hat for this part of the session. You are wearing the hat of someone who has specific expertise or experience in the area under discussion.

> Third, make sure your coachee wants the information. Ask permission even if you are certain that the coachee will say yes. Asking permission before offering suggestions preserves the integrity of the coaching relationship. And be ready for coachees to say that they'd rather find out on their own.

> Fourth, be clear that you are offering this without attachment. The moment you believe you have the right answer or the right way, you have begun to impose your agenda on the coachee's action. Be clear that you are offering this with no strings attached.

Another area in which to establish clarity involves the design of your alliance with the coachee. In some cases, coachees will choose a coach specifically because that coach has relevant experience. They hire a coach who they believe understands their world, knows how things work, and understands how to be successful. When that is the case, it is important to talk about the difference between a coaching role and a consulting or mentoring role so that they know what to expect. Both coachee and coach should continue to revisit the design of the relationship as necessary as the coaching proceeds.

Let's be clear. Sometimes, in addition to managers wanting to *give* the answer, employees simply want to *get* the answer. It's safer than making decisions on their own. There's no risk in "doing what my manager told me to do"—but there's no learning, either. And it is in the learning that the team and organization stand to benefit the most. That's why it is important to key an eye on the nature of the conversation you are in. Yes, of course there will be times when a direct, simple answer or bit of advice is correctly called for; just notice when it is an unconscious default.

Distinctions for Consulting, Coaching, and Mentoring

There are certainly ways that consulting, coaching, and mentoring overlap. The bottom line is that all three approaches are designed to improve performance in a developmental process based on a working relationship. Many of the same skills apply to the coach, consultant, or mentor. In fact, there are many ways to define these three approaches and, in the end, still have room for discussion about the finer points. Our goal here is to see generally how the process and relationships differ.

Consulting

A consulting relationship focuses on achieving a particular outcome. The consultant provides analysis and a proposed process. The consultant brings experience, training, and expertise in a particular area that matches the requirements necessary to achieve results. Once the stated goal is achieved, the relationship is complete. These relationships tend to be formal—contracted for a specific time frame. Because of the professional, contractual nature of the work. we tend to say *consultant and client* rather than *coach and coachee*. The consultant is the authority in the relationship.

Coaching

In a coaching relationship, there is attention given to outcomes, of course. Accountability for results is key to a coaching process. But the focus of the relationship is on the coachee, and the issues become the ways coachees develop, grow, and make better choices. We should be clear that here we are describing *co-active coaching* relationships. There are other coaching forms. It is still possible in some organizations to hear a manager say to an employee, "I have some coaching for you." In that case, the intended outcome is correction, not development.

In a coaching relationship, it's not necessary that the coach have expertise or background in the coachee's area of interest or the topic at hand. What the coach brings to the relationship is expertise in coaching skills rather than content knowledge. In fact, a lack of expertise about the subject can benefit the working relationship between coach and coachee because there is less tendency to get drawn into details of a content issue and lose the personal development.

As we have described throughout the book, coaching can be both a formal, professional relationship between the coach and the coachee and a less formal relationship between the leader, manager, or supervisor and an employee or team member. These informal coaching relationships start to blur the line between coaching and mentoring.

Mentoring

A mentoring relationship focuses more on personal development than on problem solving or goal achievement. One of the main differences between coaching and mentoring is a difference in level of expertise or experience. There is a teaching and modeling role for the mentor and, as a consequence, a difference in rank. There is a way that mentorees "look up" to their mentor as a source of wisdom and for guidance. The two people are usually in the same field, are typically in the same company, and are often on similar career trajectories. There is an underlying purpose of career development for the mentoree.

In our co-active coaching model, we described in chapter 2 how both the coach and coachee grant power to the relationship. The two are peers for the benefit of the coachee. In a mentoring relationship, there is a way that mentorees grant power to their mentor. Even so, the connection is typically quite personal.

Mentoring relationships can also be more formal or less formal. Some organizations put great emphasis on developing mentor relationships that have clearly described guidelines—sometimes with specific timelines. There are also informal mentoring relationships where two people connect and stay in that mentoring relationship for a long time.

Co-active Relationships in All Three Cases

The form and purpose, the focus for development, and the process may differ, but the foundational nature of co-active relationship applies in all three cases. Underneath the structure is a co-commitment to listening, caring, and collaborating. There is an equality of intent and alignment that supports the relationship. Whether it is formally done or not, there is an implied alliance between the two people involved in consulting, coaching, or mentoring relationships. When leaders tune in to the deeper conversation, they respond at a deeper level and with more agility to dance with these three different modalities. The response in the moment is guided by what will serve this particular person and situation.

Therapy and Coaching

Coaching can absolutely have a therapeutic effect, but it is not therapy. The confusion happens when coaches assume that emotion is the realm of therapy and that they need to steer away quickly whenever emotion shows up. Rational discourse is safer. Actually, as we observed in process coaching, emotions are an inseparable part of the human experience.

If we don't make that rule about emotion, there are more ways that counseling and coaching overlap, especially with some contemporary therapy modalities. What does seem clear is that, in general, therapists are trained to diagnose emotional problems and work with clients to heal the emotional wounds; coaches are not trained to diagnose and do not focus on healing. Counseling and coaching have different underlying purposes. The distinction may be subtle in some cases, especially when coaches are in the realm of process coaching.

Regardless of the finer points of definition, it is true that when coachees in coaching make courageous choices in their lives, they often experience a sense of healing, of breaking old patterns and old bonds, of stepping out of a confining box and into a new strength. Coaching, however, does not focus on the emotional issues and the relationship web that results. Emotion may be present in the conversation, but it is not the work of the coaching. As long as coaches focus on the three principles and the contexts and skills of coaching, they are very likely to stay within bounds. (The Coaches Toolkit online includes the ethical standards for professional coaches published by the International Coach Federation. *coactive.com/toolkit*)

The Coach's Commitment

Just how far are you willing to go for the sake of your coachee's fulfilling life and personal development? And at what point do you settle into a state of comfort—especially with coachees with whom you enjoy working—and find yourself supporting only a portion of their dream or holding a vision of their potential that is within reach and satisfactory but not great? At what point do you take the easier path rather than the challenging conversation?

It can happen, unconsciously, and it is a reminder that as coaches we need to be constantly vigilant, constantly holding a vision for our coachees that on some days they are not able to hold for themselves. Leaders and managers need to stay committed to the larger purpose in spite of the short-term pressures.

Coachees count on you to give them your 100 percent commitment. Be alert to those times when you begin to buy into their stories without question. Be willing to push back, to suggest a contrary point of view just for the sake of their exploration, so they are forced to be clear and rigorous in the stands they take.

When your coachees present their portrait of their world as if it is The Truth and you find yourself nodding in agreement, pause long enough to question the underlying assumptions. For example, when coachees say things like, "I'm so busy, so committed, I don't have time to X," become curious. It may be true that a coachee is too busy, but it may also be an excuse that allows this person to avoid a difficult choice that would work out best in the long run. You might wonder, *What is the coachee really committed to, after all?*

As coach, you are the model of courageous questioning. Part of your job is to be blunt—to say the unpopular, or even unreasonable, thing to help coachees reach their potential and live their fulfilling life, however they define it. If living a fulfilling life is a radical act, as we have said, then there will be times when yours will be the voice of fierce courage. You need to be willing to ask the tough question or tell the hard truth, even if it means your coachees will not like what they hear. There may be times when you must be willing to go too far and maybe even be fired. Sometimes the toughest question is for the coach: *What are you really committed to, after all?*

For managers, there is a similar imperative that sets apart leaders who are truly committed to their direct reports. And it's tricky because you have a management role that you are accountable for, in addition to the coach role you take on when that is called for. You have a responsibility to the organization to deliver results, a responsibility for clear work direction and accountability, and a responsibility to develop talent. When you step into the role of coach, the question is still the same: *What are you really committed to?*

Sample Coaching

Courageous Questioning (Coaches)

COACH: Is that your final decision?

Coachee: Yes. I'll be moving back to my hometown as soon as I can make the arrangements—maybe in a month.

COACH: I'm surprised.

Coachee: I know.

COACH: Look, Kathy, it's your life. You have to choose what you think is best, but as your coach and someone who really believes in you, I have to say I'm confused.

Coachee: And a little irritated, it sounds like. You think I'm selling out again.

COACH: Don't you?

Coachee: I'm tired of fighting.

COACH: I understand. I've seen you battle. I've seen you face the rejection letters, work the part-time job, write late into the night. I've seen that struggle. Where did that determination come from?

Coachee: Maybe I was just fooling myself.

COACH: I'm going to push back here. You tell me if I go too far.

Coachee: It just seems so hopeless.

COACH: I don't remember "hope" on your list of values. I remember the dream. I remember the woman who came to this city filled with fire and determination, taking a stand for her life and believing in herself.

Coachee: I was pretty wide-eyed.

COACH: I remember lots of doubt, too. Days when you were down. I don't believe the fire has gone out. I just don't believe it.

Coachee: The money's almost gone. My job is boring. I'm not having any fun. This is not the dream I signed up for.

COACH: I understand that, and I have a request: take a break from the writing, but don't take any action about moving. Will you do that?

Coachee: But if I'm not writing, what's the point? I'm just punching a clock.

COACH: You're tired. The dream is tired, too. Give it a rest. When we talk next week, we can see how you're doing. Are you willing? You can say no and I'll let it go, but I'm truly asking on your behalf—on behalf of the person who believes she was born to write.

Coachee: Yes. Okay. For that person.

Courageous Questioning (Leaders and Managers)

Employee: You said you wanted to talk.

MANAGER: I do.

Employee: It sounds ominous. Should I be worried?

MANAGER: I saw your email to Ellen about the Stargazer project.

Employee: Yeah. We're behind schedule and can't seem to get caught up. I'm not likely to meet my personal KPI at this rate.

MANAGER: Hitting the targets is important, no question, but I'm more concerned right now about you and your role than I am about the schedule.

Employee: You've seen the reports . . . supplier problems, problems with IT, unexpected costs . . .

MANAGER: All of that is true. This project has had more than its share of surprises. But what I wanted to talk about is your role. This could be a real career-advancing opportunity. We picked you especially for your ability—and history—of handling projects like this. Do this: shift from the problems on the project for a minute, and focus on yourself. What is it you really want?

Employee: A successful project, obviously. Recognition for that and a chance at promotion.

MANAGER: From outside, it looks like you are getting in your own way. I have not lost my faith in you. I'm still committed. My question for you would be, "What are you committed to?"

Employee: There are all these different people, different demands, deadlines. I'm trying to keep everyone on board, happy, productive.

MANAGER: . . . And what are you committed to?

Employee: Maybe I'm working too hard to be liked, and not enough on being effective.

MANAGER: So what would that look like?

Integration

As we said early in the book, a co-active conversation is a dance. And the music is constantly changing. There are steps to learn and practice, and we have covered them and provided exercises to help you become a better dancer. Putting it all together is an integration process that happens in real life—not by reading about it.

If you are starting down this coaching skills path, embrace the fact that there is a learning curve. You will become more competent by embracing your own incompetence and by learning from every experience.

Fundamentally, that is the realm we are inviting our coachees and employees into. We make it as safe as possible, knowing it will likely be uncomfortable and it won't be a straight line—there will be forward movement and backtracking. That's the nature of learning.

The result is worth it for both the coach and coachee. One of the less obvious, but important, qualities of a co-active relationship is the way both benefit by growing in this alliance.

CHAPTER 12

The Expanding World of Coaching

The Expanding World of Coaching

In the years since the first edition of this book was published, coaching has entered the mainstream of life and work, on every continent and in nearly every aspect of life. Where it once focused on two main categories, personal coaching for individuals and executive coaching for corporate executives and managers, today it has evolved and spun off into hundreds of variations and hybrids.

You will find coaches working with individuals at every stage of life and in different life circumstances. Coaches now work in niches as diverse as teenagers preparing for college, graduates exploring career choices, couples considering marriage, individuals relocating or retiring, and patients facing life-altering or terminal illnesses. Coaches may specialize in working with certain groups, such as senior executives, engineers, doctors, artists and musicians, teachers, at-risk teens, or directors and volunteers at nonprofit organizations.

Some coaches combine their work with other interest areas, including outdoor activities such as river rafting and rock climbing, where the activity itself is like a living metaphor for coaching with goal setting and accountability. There are coaches who specialize in financial planning, public speaking, time management, and weight loss and fitness work. Many coaches combine coaching with related services that might include strategic planning, communications training, or leadership development.

In this book, we have emphasized individual, one-on-one coaching, but one of the fastest-growing segments of the coaching profession includes team coaching for work teams and relationship coaching for couples, partnerships, and families. All of the principles, contexts, and coaching skills still apply, but the "coachee" is the team or the relationship. The team or relationship is a living system with personality and values; there are clearly team goals different from the combined goals of individual team members. A team really is more than the sum of the parts.

And yet the team also consists of all of the individual personalities, priorities, attitudes, and desires of team members. As organizations put more and more emphasis on teams to deliver productivity improvement, this is a coaching niche that will continue to expand. Coaching teams is inherently more complex, and it requires specialized skills and competencies and an aptitude for group dynamics. It can be chaotic, emotional, demanding, and inspiring.

In addition to the obvious professional coach practitioner, the expanding world of coaching includes workplace coach professionals, and as we have seen in the dialogue examples, it includes coaching skills used by managers and leaders in their everyday life at work.

Today coaching represents a global industry that generates more than $2 billion annually and is a major support system for leaders, managers, and entrepreneurs. We have seen the profession grow and attract dedicated professionals; we have seen the commitment to establish and maintain high-quality and ethical standards; we have trained tens of thousands of coaches around the world; and we have witnessed the profession make an enormous difference in the lives of individuals and the performance of organizations. Without question, coaching over the last two decades has earned a respected place as a credible, proven support system for change that is uniquely customized to each coachee.

Coachee Relationships

For coaches working with individuals or teams in organizations, the relationship has an added layer beyond just coach and coachee that needs to be addressed. It is the three-way dynamic created between the coach, the coachee, and the organization. In this case, the coach needs to design a three-way alliance. Issues of confidentiality must be defined and roles clarified. Does the organization expect a report from the coach or the coachee? Who sets the goals and criteria for the coaching—coachee or organization? If coaching is to be effective, there must be a sincere commitment on the part of the coachee; otherwise, the work may merely be a way of exerting pressure on compliance.

Some organizations insist that the coaching focus only on performance goals; in other organizations, coaches are empowered to help coachees clarify and pursue the most fulfilling and motivating personal path, even if these individuals end up leaving the organization. There is tremendous power in an organization that is fueled by fully motivated employees, and many organizations are aware that unmotivated employees are a drain on momentum.

Workplace Coaches

We know from experience that the co-active coaching model works as effectively with workplace coaches working inside organizations as it does with external coach practitioners. We have years of feedback from workplace coaches in large and small companies, agencies, and nonprofit organizations around the world. We also know that there are certain differences that must be addressed in order for the coaching to be effective.

Here again, a three-way dynamic is at play among the workplace coach, the coachee, and the organization or sponsor. The situation can be quite sensitive, and in our experience, the best approach is to establish clarity of roles and expectations in the early design of the coaching alliance involving all three parties. It is especially important for workplace coaches to be clear about the boundaries for the coaching relationship.

Coaching as a Complement to Other Work

Change that takes root happens over time and is most likely to be sustained with attention and support. Coaching is an ideal complement to program changes and a beneficial follow-up for activities or experiences designed to open up new insight or learning. A workshop, seminar, or off-site retreat can have extraordinary impact, but that impact may easily fade as individuals are separated from the experience over time.

Coaching keeps the learning alive; in fact, it nourishes the seeds that were planted in that initial experience. Consultants and team leaders are turning to coaching more and more as a means of sustaining change. Experiential trainers and program leaders are incorporating ongoing coaching in order to continue the work that began in the initial adventure or experience.

Every system—human and natural—resists change. Homeostasis is a compelling power that tends to keep things as they are and exerts pressure to return to the way things have always been. There is also a complementary urge for change in every system, but in the human world it seems to need a fair amount of encouragement and support. Coaching is an ideal mechanism for sustaining change.

So Many Options

We know we have barely scratched the surface of the wide range of possibilities for coaches. There are many books and other resources available for coaches who are looking at launching a practice. The key, in our experience, is to be very clear about your niche, your passion, and your sense of mission. You will be most successful, and most inspired, when working with the people you care about most.

And for yourself, remember you are standing on the core principles of coaching, so design your offering so that it is fulfilling—so that it resonates with your values and provides balance in your own life. Make it a design that allows you to love and live in the moment. In other words, let your practice be what you preach.

Coaching Skills for a Different Conversation

Coaching is more than a profession. It is also a communication medium with ground rules and expectations for conversation. This form of communication is also finding its way into business meetings, leadership courses, dialogue between teachers and children, and within families. Coaching emphasizes open listening, mutual respect, clarity, and willingness to engage with even difficult and emotional conversations. Daniel Goleman, with his work on emotional intelligence, paved the way for broad acceptance of this world of open communication, especially the crucial importance of emotional intelligence as a necessary quality for effective leaders. Today, the skills we most associate with professional coaching are finding their way into all sorts of conversations.

This is particularly evident in the world of work. Not only are coaching skills showing up more often in leaders and managers, but also more and more organizations are investing in training in those skills. There is an awareness that the transformative power of coaching in organizations is not just about learning skills or even the practice of using those skills from time to time for leaders and direct reports. Ultimately, the power comes from creating a coaching culture.

Imagine a World

Back in 1998, we wrote about a world we imagined; a world where coaching and coaching skills were a natural part of human relationship. That vision still holds today, but we have a growing sense that what we only imagined then is more and more a real part of the world we experience today.

Those of us who have trained coaches and coached coachees know the extraordinary impact that coaching can have on people's lives. It's why we can take a stand with such assurance for transformative change. We have seen it so often in our coachees. We've felt it in our own lives as well. Now extrapolate from that handful of people in one person's coaching circle to a whole world where coaching is part of everyday life.

Imagine a world where the fundamental skills and approach of coaching are widely used—not just by coaches, but by everyone. What if people everywhere simply assumed that the principles of fulfillment, balance, and process were a basic expectation for everyone? What if what we take for granted in coaching relationships found its way into everyday life? Imagine what that would be like.

In this world where fundamental coaching principles abound, people would be committed to fulfilling lives and work. They would be less likely to tolerate second-rate lives and more likely to decide they wouldn't settle for anything less than a full way of living that used their talents and skills completely. Children would learn that fulfillment is not something that will happen for some people someday when they are rich or famous, but is available in this moment, and every moment that follows, for those who are on a path of fulfillment.

Imagine a world where everyone has a compelling vision of his or her work: a sense of choice and purpose. Imagine a world of passionate, committed people determined to make a difference in the lives of others as they live life fully themselves. This would be a world that receives everybody's best effort, everybody's gift—instead of merely their compliance, their bodies sitting at desks, working at machines, or standing behind counters with 10 percent of their brains engaged.

Although people might be in the same exact jobs in our imagined world, they would have an entirely different frame of reference, a different attitude as they wake up in the morning. The value of work would change because it would no longer be about what job you have but about the difference you make and the values you honor in the work you do.

Imagine a world where the axioms of coaching operate everywhere: in interpersonal relationships, work dynamics, international relations. Imagine the difference it would make if people designed the alliance before embarking on a business project or a relationship. What would it be like if people routinely told the truth to one another—even the hard truth—and insisted on nothing less than that without feeling the need to erect defenses? Imagine how our political system would change if people felt free to simply tell the truth.

Imagine what would be possible if co-active conversations were the norm at work, in our families, in our schools, and maybe especially in governments around the world. Conversations of honesty, respect, curiosity, and commitment, where people listened deeply to see and be seen in our humanity and where action came from that reservoir of common caring.

Imagine a world where people are committed to truly listen, not only to the words but also to everything behind the words. What if we held out the biggest picture possible of what we and our children could be, instead of pointing out everybody's limitations? What if we came to expect greatness instead of failure or inadequacy, and treated failure, when it happens, not as a disgrace but as a form of fast learning? What if we acknowledged people's strengths instead of picking at their flaws?

This would be a world of curiosity and wonder and listening in extraordinary ways. It would be a world in which we hold one another to account for what we say we will do, expecting the best effort. In this world, we would be as committed to the truth about ourselves as we were to the truth we told others.

In this world, learning and growth would be valued over comfort and appearance. Imagine a world of compelling visions set loose to create and prosper, totally supported, totally encouraged, totally celebrated. This would be a transformative world indeed.

Glossary

Accountability. Accountability is your coachee being responsible for following through on their agreements or commitments. It stems from three questions: (1) What are you going to do? (2) When will you have this done? (3) How will you be accountable? Accountability does not include blame or judgment. Rather, the coach helps coachees to hold themselves accountable to their vision or commitment and asks them to account for the results of their intended actions to themselves, to another person or support in their lives, or on occasion, to the coach.

Acknowledgment. Acknowledgment addresses the self and who coachees had to be in order to accomplish the action they took or the awareness they achieved. It is the articulation of your deep knowing of the other. Acknowledgment has the coachee feel seen and known.

> *"I acknowledge the courage it took for you to show up for this session, knowing that you had difficult things to share with me today."*

Agenda: Big agenda. The big agenda is the meta-view, or how the coachee's choices and actions relate to their big-picture agendas. This is where coachees learn more deeply about how they operate. At its core, the big agenda consists of the three principles of co-active coaching: fulfillment, balance, and process. It assumes that coachees want these three things: (1) to live fulfilling lives, (2) to be in balance about those lives, and (3) to be present in the process of life. The coach interacts with coachees holding this big agenda at all times.

Agenda: Little agenda. The little agenda consists of the small picture, the circumstances in the coachee's life, his or her agenda of the moment. This agenda is focused on a particular event, on the coachee's choices around that event, or on the actions the coachee will take related to that specific event.

Articulating what's going on. This skill involves telling coachees what you notice about their words or their actions. It may be what you're hearing with your Level II listening, or you may name what they have not said based on your Level III listening and awareness. Sometimes, it is powerful to simply repeat the coachee's words back to them so they can really hear themselves.

> *"Michael, I know how much you say you want to change your relationship with your manager, but what I'm hearing sounds like the same old response—feeling disempowered but not speaking up."*

Asking permission. This skill enables coachees to grant the coaching relationship access to unusually intimate or sometimes uncomfortable areas of focus.

> *"May I tell you a hard truth?" "Are you willing to be coached about this sensitive issue?" "Although it may be uncomfortable, may I tell you what I am noticing?"*

Bottom-lining. This is the skill of brevity and succinctness on the part of both the coach and the coachee. It is also about encouraging coachees to get to the essence of their communication rather than engaging in long descriptions or stories.

Brainstorming. Using this skill, coach and coachee together generate ideas, alternatives, and possible solutions without judging or discussing. Some may be outrageous and impractical. This is a creative exercise to expand the possibilities available to coachees. Coach and coachee are not attached to any of the ideas suggested.

Challenge. A challenge is a request that stretches coachees way beyond their self-imposed limits and shakes up the way they see themselves. A challenge, like a request, includes three parts: (1) a specified action that is in line with the coachee's agenda, (2) conditions of satisfaction, and (3) a date or time of completion. Coachees will respond to a challenge with a yes, a no, or a counteroffer. Frequently, the counteroffer is greater than the commitment they initially intended to make.

> A coachee wants to make cold calls to increase his business. He thinks he can make only one call a day. You challenge him: *"I challenge you to make fifty calls a day!"* The coachee counteroffers with *"I'll make seven."*

Championing. Championing coachees means standing up for them when they doubt or question their abilities. Despite the coachee's self-doubt, the coach knows clearly who they are and that they are capable of much more than they think, and the coach lets the coachee know this, helping the coachee to see themselves and their capabilities more clearly.

Clarifying. When coachees are unable to articulate clearly what they want or where they are going, the coach offers clarification. Clarifying may be used in response to the coachee's vague sense of the desired outcome, confusion, or uncertainty. This skill represents a synergistic application of questioning, reframing, and articulating what is going on. It is particularly useful during the discovery process.

Clearing. Clearing is a skill that can benefit either the coachee or the coach. When coachees are preoccupied with a situation or a mental state that interferes with their ability to be present or take action, the coach assists by being an active listener while they vent or complain. Both coachee and coach hold the intention of clearing the emotionality from the situation. This active listening allows coachees to temporarily clear the situation out of the way and focus on taking the next step. When a coach gets hooked by a coachee interaction or is preoccupied with issues that do not pertain to the coachee, the coach can clear. The coach clears by sharing his or her experience or preoccupation with a colleague or a friend in order to show up and be fully present with the coachee. Clearing is time-limited, and the coach does not need to interact with the content of what the coachee is sharing—it is simply intended to clear the space so that the coachee and coach can both be present to the coaching.

Dancing in this moment. Coaches are dancing in this moment when they are being completely present with the coachee, holding the coachee's agenda, accessing their intuition, letting the coachee lead them. When coaches dance in this moment, they are actively partnering with the coachee and coaching in alignment with the coachee's direction and flow.

Designed alliance. Both coachee and coach are intimately involved in designing the coaching relationship that will be most beneficial to the coachee. Coaches and coachees begin designing their alliance during the discovery session. Designed alliances are meant to be revisited regularly as the coaching relationship and the coachee's needs tend to shift over time.

Goal setting. Coachees live into their big agendas by setting goals and following through. Goals keep a coachee focused and on track toward the person they are becoming. Goals are not the same as action; they are the desired results of action. In co-active coaching, a SMART goal is specific, measurable, accountable, resonant, and thrilling.

Granting relationship power. The coaching relationship is separate from the coachee and the coach. Because the power of coaching resides in the relationship between coach and coachee, not with either of the two individuals, both coach and coachee take responsibility for creating the coaching relationship that will most fully serve the coachee, thereby granting power to the relationship.

Holding the coachee's agenda. When coaches hold the coachee's agenda, they let go of their own biases, opinions, judgments, and answers in support of facilitating the coachee's fulfillment, balance, and process. Coaches follow the coachee's lead without knowing the right answer, giving solutions, or telling the coachee what to do. Holding the coachee's agenda requires the coach to put their whole attention on the coachee and the coachee's agenda, not on their own agenda for the coachee.

Holding the focus. Once coachees have determined a direction or a course of action, the coach's job is to keep them on track and true to that course. Coachees frequently become distracted by events in their lives, by the fears or confusion that come with big changes, or simply by the wealth of available options. The coach consistently reminds coachees of their focus and helps redirect their energy back to their desired vision, outcomes, and life choices.

Homework inquiry. When the coach gives the coachee a powerful question as homework, the intent is to deepen the coachee's learning and provoke further reflection. While an inquiry can sometimes be answered immediately, coachees are asked to consider the inquiry between sessions or over a longer period of time and to see what occurs for them. The inquiry is usually based on a particular situation that coachees are addressing at the time. An inquiry has multiple answers, none of which is "right."

> *"What are you tolerating?" "What is it to be undaunted?" "What is challenge?"*

Intruding. On occasion, the coach may need to intrude, to interrupt or wake up coachees who are caught in an old or repetitive narrative. The coach does this for the sake of the coachee's agenda, often pointing the coachee in a specific direction: *"Stop a moment. What's at the heart of this?"* Intrusion is considered rude in some cultures. In co-active coaching, however, intrusion is viewed as being direct with the coachee, allowing the coachee to honestly assess and immediately deal with the situation. Sometimes the intrusion is a hard truth:

> *"You are kidding yourself."* Or the intrusion could simply be a question about what is going on, such as *"What is most important about what you're describing?"*

> There are many ways a coach can intrude: *"Let's pause here—what do you really want?" "STOP! This is not serving you."*

Intuiting. Intuiting is the process of accessing and trusting one's inner knowing. Intuition is direct knowing, unencumbered by the thinking mind. The process of intuiting is nonlinear and not rational. Sometimes the information received through intuiting does not make logical sense to the coach; however, it is usually quite valuable to the coachee. Intuiting involves taking risks and trusting your gut. The coach offers the intuition to the coachee and must be willing to let it go if the coachee doesn't have a connection to it.

"I have a hunch that . . . "

"I sense that . . . "

"This may seem off-topic, yet as I listen to you describe your situation, the image of a lion comes to mind. Does that have any meaning to you?"

Listening. The coach listens for the coachee's vision, values, commitment, and purpose as expressed in words and demeanor. To listen for, is to listen in search of something. The coach listens with consciousness, with a purpose and focus that come from the alliance designed with the coachee. The coach is listening for the coachee's agenda, rather than thinking about their own agenda for the coachee. In co-active coaching, when coaches listen to their own thoughts, judgments, and opinions about the coachee's story, they're listening at Level I; listening that focuses on the coachee is Level II, and global listening is Level III. Co-active coaches listen at Level II and Level III when they're coaching.

Making distinctions. Coachees may feel disempowered because they have blended together two or more separate concepts, facts, or ideas. Distinguishing between the blended items helps coachees to see their situation from a fresh perspective and connects them more fully to their own resourcefulness. For example, the coachee may have blended two facts together into one disempowering belief. The belief appears to be a fact of life, but it's not.

"I am a failure because I wasn't promoted." (equating failing with failure)

"Making money means I'm successful." (equating money with success)

"If I ask for help, people will think I'm not capable." (equating asking for help with being incompetent or helpless)

Metaphor. Metaphors are used to illustrate a point and paint a verbal picture for the coachee. A metaphor can be more effective than a long or detailed explanation.

"You're almost at the finish line. Go for it! You can win the race!"

"You've been driving in neutral. What would happen if you changed gears?"

"You are the glue that holds this group together."

Meta-view. The meta-view is the big picture or expanded perspective. The coach pulls back (or asks coachees to pull back) from a coachee's immediate issues and reflects back to coachees what the coach sees through the clarity of that expanded perspective.

> *"If your whole career were like a road, and we were to take a helicopter ride up above it, what would we see when we look at this moment?"*

Perspective. Perspective is one of the gifts that the coach brings to the coaching relationship—not the "right" perspective, simply other points of view. Part of coaching is inviting coachees to experience certain issues, or even their whole lives, from different angles. When coachees see things from only one perspective, they are less resourceful and may feel victimized by their circumstances. When they are able to reexamine their viewpoints, to explore certain issues or their lives from different angles, they are more empowered to move forward. Shifting perspective can dramatically open up a coachee's sense of possibility. It is especially effective when a coachee is feeling stuck in a situation or circumstance.

Planning. The coach helps coachees articulate the direction they wish to take and actively partners with the coachee to monitor their progress. Coachees frequently benefit from support in planning and time management as the coach helps them develop their skills in these areas.

Powerful questions. A powerful question evokes clarity, action, discovery, insight, or commitment. It creates greater possibility, new learning, or clearer vision. Powerful questions are open-ended questions that do not elicit a yes-or-no response. They are derived from holding the coachee's agenda and either forwarding the coachee's action or deepening his or her learning.

> *"What do you want?" "What's next?" "How will you start?" "What does that cost you?" "What's important for you to remember?"*

Reframing. With reframing, the coach provides coachees with another perspective by taking the original information and interpreting it in a different way.

> A coachee has just been informed that she was the second choice for a high-powered position in a very competitive market. She is disappointed and is questioning her professional competence. The coach reframes the situation by pointing out that being second choice in such a competitive market indicates the high quality of the coachee's expertise and experience.

Requesting. One of the most potent coaching skills is that of making a request of the coachee. The request, based on the coachee's agenda, is designed to forward the coachee's action. The request includes a specified action, conditions of satisfaction, and a date or time for completion. There are three possible responses to a request: (1) yes, (2) no, or (3) a counteroffer. The coach is not attached to which response the coachee chooses. Any one of the coachee's three possible responses will create an opportunity to further explore the coachee's learning.

Saboteur. The saboteur concept embodies a group of thought processes and feelings that maintains the status quo in our lives and our work. It is often most apparent when change is imminent or risk-taking is occurring. The saboteur often appears to be a structure that protects us, but in fact it prevents us from moving forward and getting what we truly want. The saboteur will always be with us. It is neither good nor bad; it just is. The saboteur loses its power over us when we can identify it for what it is, notice our options in the situation, and then consciously choose the action we really want at that time.

Self-management. This skill involves the coach's ability to put aside their own biases, opinions, preferences, judgments, and beliefs in order to hold the coachee's agenda. Self-management occurs when the coach is able to step out of the way of the coachee's learning and growth, staying connected to the coachee and fully holding the track for the coachee and the coachee's agenda.

Structures. Structures are devices that remind coachees of their vision, goals, or purpose or the actions they need to take immediately. Collages, calendars, messages on voice mail, and alarm clocks are some examples of structures.

Taking charge. The coach chooses and directs the path of the coaching in order to serve the coachee's agenda. Sometimes coachees become lost in their circumstances and forget what matters most to them. That's when the coach needs to remind the coachee, by taking charge to direct the coaching back to what is most meaningful to them.

Values. Values represent who you are right now. They are principles that you hold to be of worth in your life. People often confuse values with morals, but they are not the same. Values are not chosen. They are intrinsic to you and are as distinctly yours as your thumbprint.

Vision. This is a multifaceted mental image that personally defines and inspires the coachee to take action to bring that image to life. A powerful vision is compelling, exciting, and magnetic, constantly inspiring the coachee to do their best to bring it to fruition. Vision provides coachees with direction and meaning in life and is also powerfully effective at work. Holding a vision for a department can inspire the whole team.

Witnessing. Witnessing is being authentically present with the coachee. This skill creates the space for coachees to fully express themselves. When the coach witnesses the coachee's learning and growth, the coachee feels seen and known at a very deep level.

About the Authors

Henry Kimsey-House

Henry Kimsey-House, CPCC, one of the first professional coaches in the 1980s, is the cofounder and lead designer of the provocative, experiential learning programs of The Co-Active Training Institute (CTI), the world's largest coach training organization. CTI and its Co-Active philosophy have revolutionized the lives and careers of more than 60,000 managers, leaders, and coaches throughout the world. An actor since age nine, Henry honed his insights into human emotion and the narrative process through classical theatrical training and years of stage, television, and film experience. With deep conviction that education should be driven by immersive, contextually based learning rather than dry information downloads, Henry is committed to creating richly engaging and transformative learning environments. He continues to develop innovative curricula and collaborate with other dynamic thought leaders, and is also the coauthor of *Co-Active Leadership: Five Ways to Lead*, which applies the Co-Active principles to transformative leadership. He lives with his wife, Karen Kimsey-House, in the artist community of Ashland, Oregon.

Karen Kimsey-House

Karen Kimsey-House, MFA, CPCC, is a cofounder of The Co-Active Training Institute (CTI), the foremost coach training school in the world. One of the earliest recognized luminaries in the coaching profession, she founded CTI in 1992 with Laura Whitworth and Henry Kimsey-House. Together, they created the Co-Active philosophy of relationship that informs CTI's world-renowned coaching and leadership programs.

A successful entrepreneur, Karen founded a number of start-ups before embarking on her journey with CTI. Karen is the coauthor of two additional books, *Co-Active Leadership: Five Ways to Lead* with Henry Kimsey-House and *Integration: Being Co-Active in Work and in Life* with Ann Betz. Committed to pioneering co-activity in challenged environments and troubled populations, Karen continues to lead CTI programs and is a dynamic keynote speaker around the world. On a mission of global, transformative change, she lives with her husband, Henry Kimsey-House, in the artist community of Ashland, Oregon.

Phillip Sandahl

Phillip Sandahl, MCC, CTPC, is cofounder of Team Coaching International (TCI). Its mission: to bring the transformative power of coaching to teams in organizations. Sandahl and cofounder Alexis Phillips are developers of the Team Diagnostic™ team effectiveness model, a suite of four integrated assessment tools and a team coaching methodology used by thousands of teams worldwide. The original Team Diagnostic™ assessment is available in more than 20 languages, and there are now trained, certified TCI team coach/facilitators in more than 50 countries—a combination of external coach practitioners and internal HR, OD, and L&D providers.

Sandahl is also is a former senior faculty member for CTI. He has played an important role in the international growth of coaching and is a pioneer in the field of team coaching. Sandahl is an internationally recognized coach, trainer, author, and speaker.

He can be reached at *Phillip@TeamCoachingInternational.com* or through *teamcoachinginternational.com*.

Laura Whitworth

An early pioneer in the field of professional coaching, Laura Whitworth began coaching executives, entrepreneurs, and other professionals in 1988. Laura was cofounder of CTI, the Executive Coaching Summit, the Personal and Professional Coaches Association, the Association of Coach Training Organizations, the Time to Change Prison Project, and the Bigger Game Company. Laura passed away in February 2007 after a long battle with lung cancer.

Index